NASCAR®'s
Most Wanted

Other Titles in Brassey's *Most Wanted* Series

NASCAR®'s
Most Wanted

The Top 10 Book of Outrageous Drivers, Wild Wrecks, and Other Oddities

Jim McLaurin

Brassey's, Inc.

WASHINGTON, D.C.

Copyright © 2001 Brassey's, Inc.

This book is not authorized by NASCAR, the National Association of Stock Car Auto Racing, Inc., which is the exclusive owner of the trademark NASCAR®.

Published in the United States by Brassey's, Inc. All rights reserved. No part of this book may be reproduced in any manner whatsoever without written permission from the publisher, except in the case of brief quotations embodied in critical articles and reviews.

Library of Congress Cataloging-in-Publication Data

McLaurin, Jim.
    NASCAR's most wanted : the top 10 book of outrageous drivers, wild wrecks, and other oddities / Jim McLaurin.— 1st ed.
        p.   cm.
    ISBN 1-57488-358-5
    1. NASCAR (Association)—Miscellanea. 2. Stock car racing—United States—Miscellanea. I. Title

GV1033 .M395 2001
796.72'0973—dc21

                                   2001025420

Printed in Canada on acid-free
paper that meets the American National Standards
Institute Z39-48 Standard

Brassey's, Inc.
22841 Quicksilver Drive
Dulles, Virginia 20166

Designed by Pen & Palette Unlimited.
Photographs by Bryant McMurray and Pal Parker.

First Edition

10 9 8 7 6 5 4 3 2 1

Contents

List of Photographs

Preface

In writing a book that requires historical research, one is first faced with two questions: Is the information out there? Then, is it accurate?

In answer to the former, there is a wealth of lore on the subject of stock car racing. The dilemma comes when you have to determine what is fact and what is fiction, or, better, what is cake and what is icing.

The research that went into this book turned out to be a delightful but complicated task. Often, the same story was told in slightly different fashion from several different sources. For instance, Curtis Turner was once said to have won a race wearing a white silk suit instead of a driving suit. In another telling, the suit became a three-piece business suit, and the site of the race had changed from, say, Columbia to Asheville.

But there was always a nugget of truth connecting each story, so that the story, not the fabric or the location, was the important thing.

Another conundrum was one of inclusion. In a book of "top 10" lists, categories exist in which there are a baker's dozen of choices from which to choose. Why, for instance, were the Waltrip brothers and Bodine brothers not included in the "All in the Family" list? Simple. My call. If you disagree, you have every right. I am not infallible.

And then there were many noteworthy events which were left out because they simply defied categorization. It is one thing to learn that after winning the 1981 championship, Darrell Waltrip presented his boss, Junior Johnson, with the gift of a prize mule. But it is quite another to find nine more stories involving farm animals.

The definition of terms also posed a challenge. Since, for instance, a NASCAR superspeedway is now generally regarded as a paved oval track a mile or more in length, should the old dirt track in Raleigh, North Carolina, (long since gone) be included as a superspeedway merely because of its length, or as a dirt track, which were usually considerably shorter? To my thinking, it was a dirt superspeedway.

I also faced some confusion over whether to refer to NASCAR's top division as Winston Cup, Grand Nationals, or Strictly Stock. Since NASCAR's inception, its top division has been called all three names. I tried to remain true to the time frame for each re-naming; just remember that all three are considered the division in which the big dogs ran.

Despite all the mitigating factors, this was a marvelous subject to dig around in. It left me with a much deeper appreciation of the history of the sport and an admiration of the people who have chronicled it. I hope it does the same for you.

By the way, I'd like to think that Curtis Turner's suit was pure white silk.

There are two people I would like to thank especially for their help in the preparation of this book.

First and foremost is my friend Greg Fielden. Greg is NASCAR's most noted historian and one of its truest gentlemen. When I undertook this project, I had no idea of the amount of intensive research it would require. The first place I turned was to his books. Greg has written eight volumes (maybe more; I have eight) on stock car racing, from its infancy to its "modern era," and they were invaluable.

Mostly, though, what I appreciate from Greg is this: One day when I was bogged down over the task of "borrowing" driver quotes—some from drivers long gone—from other sources, I gave him a call. "Heck, man, use what you want," he said, giving me permission to borrow freely from his work. Not only was a great burden lifted, but, I think, a book saved.

Second, I would like to thank my wife, Inez, for giving up our home computer (a device she dearly loves) for the better part of three months. And for keeping the coffee hot. And for taking out the trash. And for putting up with a pretty surly guy when things weren't going well.

"Wish I Hadn't Done That"

History has shown that race car drivers, like everybody else, are not infallible. Some, however, made bigger mistakes than others. A few of the more noted missteps in NASCAR history:

1. HERSHEL MCGRIFF

Eccentric millionaire Carl Kiekhafer plunged into racing so suddenly that he started his first season without a driver. When he showed up at Daytona in 1955 with a ton of money and plenty of good race cars, NASCAR president Bill France, Sr., recommended a driver named Hershel McGriff.

McGriff, who had a timber business in Oregon, turned Kiekhafer down. Although McGriff would enjoy modest success in a number of other series, he would never rise to stardom in the Grand National Series.

The driver Kiekhafer hired instead, Tim Flock, won 18 of 38 races in 1955 and wound up in the National Motorsports Press Association Hall of Fame.

2. **NED JARRETT**

Two-time champion Ned Jarrett wanted to end his driving career in a blaze of glory. Instead, he went out in a puff of smoke.

Jarrett, the 1965 champion, announced his retirement with little fanfare the day of the 1966 American 500 at Rockingham, North Carolina. Jarrett wanted to go out as a champion, and since the American 500 was the final race of the season, he figured he'd be the champ until it was over. It was not a farewell he'd remember without some discomfiture.

During the race, Jarrett unfastened his shoulder harness to reach outside to wipe the windshield of his #11 Ford and accidentally set off the fire extinguisher. The cockpit filled with fire extinguisher fog and he was forced to pit.

"That stuff about gagged me," Jarrett said after the race. "It also embarrassed me."

3. **CALE YARBOROUGH**

The Nashville 420 on August 25, 1973, was not exactly in Cale Yarborough's hip pocket, but he couldn't blame anyone else for his failure to win.

On lap 261, Yarborough was leading the race *under the caution* flag after a wreck when he inexplicably veered into the inside retaining wall. Yarborough had led for 126 laps when he piled it up. After he spent 14 laps in the pits for repairs, he was history.

"I guess I just forgot what I was doing," he said.

Buddy Baker took advantage of Yarborough's misfortune, leading from there on out and winning the race by four laps.

4. DAVID PEARSON

Several factors entered into David Pearson's departure from the famous Wood Brothers team after the CRC Chemicals Rebel 500 at Darlington in 1979, but Pearson didn't help his case any.

On lap 302 of the 367-lap race, Pearson pitted for tires and fuel. The fuel he got right. On the tires, he was off by two.

After the crew had changed the tires on the right side of the car, Pearson bolted out of the pit stall, only to discover that it was intended to be a four-tire stop. Since the lug nuts were taken off the left side at the same time the right side tires were going on, he made it no farther than the end of pit road before both wheels on the left side of his car fell off.

Crew chief Leonard Wood had apparently yelled, "Whoa, whoa!" and Pearson thought he said, "Go, go!"

5. RICHARD PETTY

Even the winningest driver in Winston Cup history was susceptible to occasional brain-lock.

Richard Petty was engaged in a hot battle with Bobby Allison in the 1971 Southern 500 at Darlington that ultimately proved too hot for Petty.

Allison and Petty were the only two cars on the lead lap when Petty ducked into the pits for a drink of water during a caution period. His crew apparently thought he needed gas, so they unfastened the gas cap. When he roared back onto the track before his crew could refuel the car, NASCAR black-flagged him and he was forced to return to his pit to get the cap tightened.

Allison took a one-lap victory and Petty finished second.

6. **CALE YARBOROUGH, AGAIN**

Cale Yarborough may have been the hardest charger in NASCAR history, but when it was time to quit, well, he quit. One day he misjudged quitting time by a lap.

Yarborough and Richard Petty were racing for the win in the 1984 Pepsi 400 at Daytona. Doug Heveron spun out with two laps to go, bringing out the caution flag. With the race unlikely to be restarted, Yarborough and Petty raced for the yellow flag that would lock in their positions.

Petty beat Yarborough by a foot, and Yarborough, thinking the race was over, drove to his pit on the final lap. That allowed Harry Gant to take second place. Yarborough finished third.

On the brighter side, it was Petty's 200th—and final—victory.

7. **FRED LORENZEN**

In one of the qualifying races for the 1965 Daytona 500, Fred Lorenzen passed Junior Johnson on the 39th lap. When the flagman waved the white flag to signal one lap to go, Lorenzen slowed down.

He thought it was the checkered flag, and Johnson benefited from Lorenzen's unintentional largesse. Lorenzen finished second.

Lorenzen did get a measure of revenge, however. Two days later, he won the Daytona 500 for the only time in his career.

8. **ERNIE MOORE**

Ernie Moore was the flagman for the first race at Atlanta International Motor Speedway, and his big heart proved to be his undoing.

Moore was at the NASCAR registration building when two of his pals, Johnny Dollar and "Tiger Tom" Pistone, were trying unsuccessfully to talk the officials into allowing them to race. Moore, being a nice guy, vouched for them.

When the race was under way, Dollar's car lost a tie rod coming down the front straightaway and Pistone ran over it. The rod flew up into the flagstand, hitting Moore in the neck.

He woke up in the hospital that night, 35 stitches later, regretting his good deed.

9. DODGE "FACTORY TEAM"

Drivers and flagmen aren't the only ones who pull boners. In 1967, Bobby Allison was driving for Cotton Owens's factory Dodge team. Owens, whose car was not in the championship hunt, decided to skip the race at Oxford, Maine, on July 11.

Allison got permission from Owens, took a Chevrolet owned by J. D. Bracken up to the race, and won it by a lap over the field.

When Allison got back to his home in Alabama, he had a message waiting from the Dodge boys: "You're fired."

Allison went on to win 77 more races in his career. Only seven were in Dodges.

10. LUDIVICO SCARFIOTTI

In 1966, Italian Grand Prix winner Ludivico Scarfiotti was lured to, of all places, Rockingham, North Carolina, for the American 500.

He was a whiz on road courses but had problems getting the heavy American stock cars up to speed on the oval track. He complained to NASCAR president Bill France, Sr., who had been instrumental in getting Scarfiotti to make the trans-atlantic trip.

Fifty-seven-year-old France, long retired from competition, jumped in the car and in a few laps was averaging in the high 109-mph range, nearly equaling Scarfiotti, who had gone only 110. Scarfiotti complained no more.

Magic Time

Considering that as many as 43 drivers participate in each race, there are no undefeated drivers in racing. (At Darlington in 1951, 82 cars started the race and 81 ended up losers.) But a few drivers have risen above the fray to post exceptional seasons.

1. RICHARD PETTY, 1967

In 1967, Richard Petty's nickname changed from "The Randle-man Rocket" to "The King." Twenty-seven wins in 48 races will do that for a guy.

Petty won 11 races by the season's midpoint, then went on a tear. He won a 300-miler at Trenton, New Jersey, finished second to Bobby Allison at Oxford, Maine, then won three more in a row. He lost to Dick Hutcherson at Maryville, Tennessee, won at Nashville, fell out with engine problems at Atlanta, then went on a winning streak that bordered on the impossible. For two months, he was unbeatable, winning 10 races in a row, something accomplished neither before nor since.

Petty broke Tim Flock's record of 18 wins in a season in a 100-miler at Columbia, South Carolina. His 10-win streak ended at Charlotte in the National 500 when he blew the engine in his Plymouth, giving the victory to Curtis Turner.

2. TIM FLOCK, 1955

Carl Kiekhafer, the owner of Mercury Outboard Motors, made a lasting, if brief, impression on stock car racing. His number-one driver, Tim Flock, would do most of the impressing.

In 1955, driving a ghostly white Chrysler, Flock won 18 races in 38 starts.

Just a year earlier, Flock had quit racing, miffed that he had been disqualified on a technicality after the race on the beach at Daytona.

Kiekhafer lured him back, and Flock made it worthwhile for both. Flock won the Grand National championship by 1,508 points over Buck Baker. After the season, Kiekhafer told Flock that he could keep all the prize money ($37,799.60) he'd won, something unheard of then or now.

3. BOBBY ISAAC, 1969

Isaac never liked the big superspeedways, but he was a master of the short tracks so plentiful in NASCAR in the 1960s. In 1969, he won 17 races (10 of them from the pole, a record) and 19 pole positions. Of those wins, all but one were on tracks shorter than a mile. So were all of his pole wins, save one. Isaac's win in the inaugural Texas 500, a two-mile track in College Station, was the first superspeedway win of his career. Of his 37 career victories, all but five came on short tracks.

4. NED JARRETT, 1964-65

It is hard to put together two seasons like the ones Jarrett had in 1964 and 1965. Jarrett, the 1961 champion, won 15

Bryant McMurray

Ned Jarrett

Ned Jarrett, shown here in 1983, won two Grand
National championships before his retirement to the
broadcast booth.

races in 1964 and 13 in 1965. The latter season resulted in
his second NASCAR title.

In 1964, he won the first race of the season at Concord,
North Carolina, and the season finale almost a year to the

day later. Oddly enough, of his remaining 13 wins, he won 10 in back-to-back pairs.

One of his 13 wins in 1965 was the Southern 500 at Darlington, and he won it by a whopping 14 laps over the field. It was his only Darlington win and remains the largest margin of victory in NASCAR history.

5. JEFF GORDOn, 1998

Considering the quality of competition, Gordon's 13 wins in 1998 added up to perhaps the most phenomenal season in the history of racing. From June 28 to August 16, Gordon won six straight Winston Cup races—a phenomenal feat—and eight of nine through the Southern 500 on Labor Day weekend. He finished the season with three wins in the last four races and went out with back-to-back victories.

6. DALE EARnHARDT, 1987

His competitors should have known they were in trouble when Earnhardt dominated at Rockingham in the second race of the 1987 season. He was out to back up his second championship with a third, and he let little get in his way. Earnhardt won five of the next six races and, before the season ended, had 11 wins and the championship.

He won races but not many friends. When he slammed Sterling Marlin in the wall at Bristol, NASCAR told Earnhardt that he'd be penalized for rough driving if it happened again. He said, "Hey, this is Bristol. You've got to be aggressive to race here."

7. JUnIOR JOHnSOn, 1965

Perhaps even more remarkable than Ned Jarrett's 13 wins in 1965 were the 13 recorded by Junior Johnson that year.

Jarrett ran the full schedule of 54 races; Johnson ran in only 36, meaning that if Junior showed up, Ned had his hands full.

Johnson won a qualifying race at Daytona but did not finish five of the season's first six races. At Richmond, he backed off the throttle and won by 18 seconds. It broke a personal 10-year losing streak at the track and set the tone for the season.

"Today, I decided to take it easy and see if I could win a race on this track," he said.

8. DAVID PEARSON, 1973

David Pearson didn't have a bad part-time job in 1973, when he took over the driving duties for the famous Wood Brothers team. He competed in only 18 of 28 races that year and won 11 of them.

The Woods figured their profit margin would be better if they ran only the "big" races, eschewing the short-track circuit, and with Pearson, they were right. In the first 10 races in which he competed, he won seven and finished second once.

Pearson wound up with 11 wins and $228,408 in prize winnings, more than all but two drivers that year—and those other two competed in all 28.

9. CALE YARBOROUGH, 1974, 1978

Like most drivers who were lucky enough to get the chance, Cale Yarborough discovered he was a much better driver in Junior Johnson's cars.

Yarborough won three consecutive championships with Johnson and had 55 of his career 83 victories in Johnson's cars.

The matching of two of the hardest chargers in NASCAR history produced results. Yarborough won 10 races in both the 1974 and 1978 seasons by following Johnson's dictum: "All I want back is the steering wheel."

10. **DARRELL WALTRIP**

See Cale Yarborough, above. When Yarborough left Johnson to cut back on his racing schedule after the 1980 season, Waltrip stepped in to fill his seat.

Again, a great match. In their six-year association, Waltrip scored 43 of his 84 career wins. He won back-to-back championships in 1981 and 1982 and picked up his third title in 1985.

The first two seasons were pure magic. Waltrip won a dozen races each season, winning his first title in 1981 with a dramatic second-half performance. In the 13 races following the midseason Firecracker 400, Waltrip won seven times, finished second five times, and was third once.

Turner Tales

Curtis Turner was a legend. Period. Exclamation point. The native Virginian made and lost several fortunes in the timber business, and he raced just for the hell of it. In terms of wins, he may not have been the best driver ever on a dirt track, but he was undoubtedly the best at driving on dirt. Turner tore up a lot of race cars, but he was perhaps NASCAR's first superstar, because people loved to see him race.

Off the track, he was larger than life. He was a party animal of epic proportions, a boozer with a hollow leg and a womanizer who kept score on a chalkboard.

By the time of his death in a private plane crash in 1970, Turner had left enough stories for a book.

1. IS TROOPER SMITH HOME?

After a long night of partying with one of his "baby dolls" (Turner called all his girlfriends "Baby doll" and all men "Pops"), he was returning to his home in Charlotte when he was stopped by a North Carolina state trooper.

The trooper wrote Turner a ticket, of course, and Turner was incensed. Noting the officer's name on his badge, Turner headed for the closest gas station, looked the name up in

Curtis Turner
Curtis Turner was in a class by himself, on the track or off it. He'd wreck a driver, then invite him to one of his legendary parties that sometimes lasted for days. Nobody wanted to win more than Turner did, and certainly nobody celebrated one any better.

Pal Parker

the phone book, and had his baby doll call the trooper's house—at 2 a.m.

When the trooper's wife answered, Turner's gal said that she was tired of waiting at a certain bar and that she was going home. Then she hung up.

No doubt, both men paid a penalty for that night.

2. BETTING MAN

Turner hung with a good crowd. One night at a track somewhere north of Charlotte, one of his friends—history is unclear whether he was a doctor or a lawyer—bet Turner $500 that he couldn't lead the first lap.

Turner started in the third or fourth row, and he did lead the first lap. But it was the only one he led. He completely demolished his car getting to the front.

In the 1950s, doctors paid better than race promoters.

3. **PAPER, MISTER?**

Turner and Lee Petty weren't archenemies, but they did not get along. Petty made his living at racing and often took exception with Turner's anything-to-win style of driving.

At a race in Virginia one night, Turner had been particularly rough on equipment—his and Petty's—and after the race, Petty confronted him.

Turner was sitting on a wooden fence, taking a post-race nip, when Petty approached with a rolled-up newspaper in his hand. He mentioned Turner's transgressions, and when Turner tried to laugh them off, Petty whacked him upside the head.

Of course, the paper was a special "torque-wrench edition," and with extra heft provided by the tool, Petty got his point across.

4. **WANT A RECEIPT FOR THAT?**

Turner often bought and sold timber during the day and raced at night. Ralph Moody, the legendary mechanic from New England, was Turner's crew chief for a race one night at Winston-Salem, and when Turner showed up at the track, he had a brown envelope that he asked Moody to hang onto while he raced.

Moody stuffed the envelope in his T-shirt and didn't think anything of it. After the race, when the two got into Turner's plane to fly on to the next race, Turner asked Moody if he still had the envelope. Moody said that he did, and Turner asked him if he knew what was in it.

Moody said, "No," whereupon Turner informed him that he'd been carrying around $5 million in cash and checks under his BVDs.

5. **FRONT DOOR, PLEASE**

Turner's parties were legendary affairs, likely to go on for several days. His favorite phrase, no matter the occasion, was "There's another party startin' in about 15 minutes."

One time before a race at Rockingham, Moody said that he got a call from Turner asking him to come by to pick him up, but not to come to the back door.

It seems that Curtis had about a three-day party going on with his secretary, and the secretary's husband was out in the backyard with a rifle. Every time Turner would try to slip out the back way to the garage, the guy would fire off a couple of rounds at the door.

Moody drove to the front door, Turner sprinted to his car, and the two went to Rockingham. The next day, Turner won the race.

6. **SCHUSSING DOWN MAIN**

Turner and his pal "Little Joe" Weatherly were rough on rental cars—so rough, in fact, that Hertz sent out a bulletin instructing its offices not to give the two even a map, much less rent them a car.

In Columbia, South Carolina, one night after a race, Turner, well-oiled, had impressed his date by slaloming down a main thoroughfare, using light posts as his gates. Over the sidewalk, down onto the street, back up on the sidewalk—at 90 mph, hubcaps flying in every direction.

The "baby doll" was impressed. Hertz wasn't.

7. **CHECK YOUR OIL, TOO, MISTER?**

Although Turner and Weatherly were teammates driving for Moody, nothing delighted them better than beating and banging on each other.

At Darlington one year, Weatherly passed Turner, and Turner nearly destroyed both cars trying to get back into the lead. Moody was so irate that he radioed Turner that if he kept it up, his crew wouldn't pit him when he came in.

After a few more laps of mayhem, Turner came in for service, and Moody ordered the crew to sit on the wall. When Turner saw he wasn't getting fresh tires—much less a windshield wipe—he drove off in a rage, straight into the wall.

The next morning, according to Moody, Turner drove to the team's shop, which had roll-up doors, crashed his brand-new Cadillac through the doors, put it in reverse, backed out, and peeled rubber for half a block. Without saying a word.

8. **RETURN YOUR TRAY TABLES TO THE UPRIGHT POSITION**

This story is true, though the passenger changes depending on who is telling it: Turner was a skilled, if untutored, pilot. Once, he was late reaching Darlington; instead of flying into the local airport, he tried to land on the backstretch of the track.

Getting in was no problem; getting out was another story. The backstretch of the old track was only some 1,300 feet long, with two-story banking in the third turn to clear. Taking off would have been a daunting task even for Chuck Yeager.

The way Joe Weatherly told it, when Turner got ready to leave, he asked Little Joe if he wanted to fly with him. Little Joe agreed, of course.

Knowing it would take all his concentration to get the plane off the ground in such a short space, Turner asked Weatherly if he'd handle the landing gear.

Turner taxied through the first and second turns, then gunned it. As the plane roared down the back straightaway headed for the mountainous turn, Turner looked over at his companion and asked, "Pops, we flyin' yet?"

Weatherly, perhaps as crazy as Turner, replied, "I hope so. I lifted the landing gear a long time ago."

9. MORNIN', BOSS

Turner drove briefly for the famous Wood Brothers racing team. One morning before a race, Leonard Wood, the chief mechanic, arrived at the track to find his driver snoring in the race car, sleeping off the effects of a hard night.

Turner woke up, bid Leonard good morning, then went out and won the race. Wood wasn't surprised, but then nothing about Turner should have surprised anyone.

Turner also had another saying: "If you feel bad enough before a race, then nothing worse can happen to you."

10. "PUSH HIM"

Seven years before his death in a plane crash, Turner met and married Caroline "Bunny" Vance, 24 years his junior. If it was not love at first sight, it was close.

When Turner wooed her with roses and a 2.5 carat diamond ring, the simple country girl said she'd have to ask her mama. When her mother found out that she wanted to marry a rich and famous race-car driver, she had one question: What are you going to do when he's 80 years old and all crippled up and in a wheelchair?

Bunny's answer was simple, and it went a long way to describe the effect Turner had on people: "Push him," she said.

She got her mother's approval.

Real Racers

By its very nature, auto racing demands more from its participants than any other sport. Life and limb are in peril; the difference between success and failure can hang on a $2 part. But there are some who, on occasion, rise above those day-to-day demands.

1. DICK RATHMANN

Californian Dick Rathmann won 13 Grand National events during his brief sojourn into NASCAR, but none would ever mean as much as a 250-lapper at Oakland, California, in 1954.

Four days before the race, Rathmann and his mechanic, Jim Ellis, picked up a brand-new Hudson Hornet in Atlanta and began the long tow to California. About a hundred miles from Oakland, after driving through a snowstorm, the tow car broke down. Rathmann and Ellis used the race car for a tow car and arrived at the track at 1 a.m. on the morning of the race.

Rathmann's car was weakened by the strain of towing the tow car, and during his qualifying run, the gas tank fell off. Fortunately, another brand-new Hudson had wrecked during its time trial. Everything on it was bent or broken—except the gas tank.

Rathmann borrowed the tank and strapped it on his car. Starting from the dead-last position, Rathmann won the race. It was the first last-to-first win in NASCAR history.

When someone remarked that it took two hours, 27 minutes, and 57 seconds for him to win the race, Rathmann laughed and said it felt more like a week.

2. **CALE YARBOROUGH**

There was never a driver who wanted to race more than Cale Yarborough did. He was 11 years old when he sneaked under the fence at Darlington to see the 1951 Southern 500. He was 17 the first time he raced in it.

The trouble was, a driver had to be 21 in order to get a NASCAR license. No problem there. Yarborough had a girl-friend who worked at the courthouse. He sent NASCAR a bogus birth certificate and they sent him a license.

The NASCAR officials discovered the discrepancy and booted him out of the track. Again, no problem. The hole in the fence was still there. He sneaked back in and, by lying on the floorboards until just before qualifying and then shooing his buddy Bobby Weatherly out of the driver's seat, Yarborough qualified for the race.

In almost a Keystone Cops switcheroo, the two again traded places just before the start of the Southern 500. The charade lasted 27 laps before the same official who had kicked Yarborough out earlier noticed Weatherly standing around the pits. The official put two and two together, and Yarborough was gone for good.

For the day, at least. He would return.

3. JOE WEATHERLY

Joe Weatherly was known as the "Clown Prince of Racing," but his puckish sense of humor belied a fierce competitive nature that memorably revealed itself during the 1963 season.

Weatherly won the 1962 championship driving first-class Pontiacs owned by Bud Moore, but when General Motors pulled back its support for the 1963 season, Moore told Weatherly that he could afford to run only the major races.

So Weatherly hitched rides with eight other car owners—often driving inferior machines—and managed to race in 53 of the 54 events. Despite getting only three wins to Richard Petty's 13 (and racing in one fewer race), Weatherly's consistency on the track carried the day. He won the championship by 2,228 points (33,398-31,170) over Petty.

4. ELMO LANGLEY

Elmo Langley was not exactly a heavy hitter during his career, though he did win two races. On May 19, 1991, long after his driving career was over, he beat the best.

Prior to the running of The Winston all-star race at Charlotte Motor Speedway, series sponsor R.J. Reynolds rented Winston Cup cars, painted them up in the colors of the men who had made them famous, and put on the Winston Legends race. A special half-mile track was built on the front stretch just for the show.

Langley, who worked as a NASCAR official and pace-car driver for the Winston Cup circuit, started 16th in the 22-car field that included such driving greats as Junior Johnson, Tim Flock, and Fred Lorenzen.

Cale Yarborough took command after crashes had decimated half of the field, but on the final lap, Langley, in hot pursuit, gave Yarborough the tiniest of nudges and beat him to the checkered flag by 10 feet.

"Man, this is great," Langley said afterward. "I got to Cale on the last lap and I didn't see any reason to back off!"

5. JOHNNY BRUNER

Flagman Johnny Bruner disdained the flagstand, preferring to wave the silk from the edge of the track.

It proved to be a dangerous preference on February 2, 1952, when 61 cars lined up on the beach-road course at Daytona Beach.

Tommy Thompson of Louisville lost control of his big '51 Chrysler just a few yards short of the finish line, hit Bruner, and knocked him 10 feet in the air.

Bruner was unhurt, but he was a bit more careful playing in traffic from that day forward.

6. BOBBY WAWAK

Things were going fine for journeyman Bobby Wawak for the first two laps of the 1977 Daytona 500. Then his car erupted in flames. It was sufficiently warm for Wawak to jump out of the window while the car was still rolling—at 40 mph.

Wawak was seriously burned but managed to run to the infield infirmary. He was taken to a local hospital.

If Hollywood had written the script, Wawak would have come back and won the next race. Hollywood didn't have a say. The next time Wawak raced, in the Virginia 500 at Martinsville some two months later, he finished dead last in the 30-car field.

But he was there.

7. **CURTIS TURNER**

Curtis Turner didn't need to race for a living. He made his money selling timber. He spent it having a good time, and that happened to include racing.

A few days before a race at Columbia, South Carolina, NASCAR informed the drivers that they would be required to wear suits.

Turner showed up wearing a three-piece business suit, saying that NASCAR hadn't specified what kind of suit. He added that his sponsors wanted a gentleman driver, and the suit was a first step in that direction.

He finished third without even loosening his tie. That's a racer.

8. **RICHARD PETTY**

Don't let Richard Petty's big grin fool you: He's as tough as they come.

On May 9, 1970, Petty had what he considers the roughest wreck of his career. In the Rebel 400 at Darlington, Petty's Plymouth Roadrunner brushed the outside rail in the fourth turn, then hit the inside wall head-on, sending chunks of concrete flying. He flipped four times and was taken to the hospital unconscious. He was diagnosed as having a broken shoulder.

Even back then, there were rumors of his retirement, and the serious wreck only fueled them. Petty scoffed at the notion, getting back into his car less than a month later (June 7, 1970) at Michigan International Speedway for the Motor State 400. He would drive 686 more races before he hung up his helmet for good.

9. **CHARLIE MINCEY**

The locals took a measure of pride in Charlie Mincey's ninth-place finish in the 200-lapper at Central City Speedway in Macon, Georgia on September 12, 1954. Mincey, a hotshot modified driver from the Macon area, was running in the top five until he ran out of gas with 16 laps remaining.

His good showing against the big boys, however, was not the reason for the fans' applause. He was cheered more because he finished at all.

In the opening laps, Mincey had flipped his big Earl Brooks' Oldsmobile. The car landed on all four wheels and Mincey had kept on going.

10. **JOE WEATHERLY, AGAIN**

Bobby Wawak was not the only driver ever to bring in a smoker. Joe Weatherly did it 21 years earlier and, as usual, with flair.

On May 12, 1956, at Raleigh Speedway, Weatherly was riding among the front-runners in a 200-lap Convertible Division race when his '56 Ford erupted in flames.

Weatherly didn't abandon his car, so Ralph Liguori slowed down and gave him a push to the pits. It got warm enough for Weatherly to stand up in the seat, but he drove it all the way in.

Famous Comebacks

It's one thing to succeed the first time around, but the true test of character often doesn't come until life has knocked you down a couple of times. That is not to say the drivers below all won. But they did try.

1. HERB THOMAS

Two-time champion Herb Thomas had been written off for the season following a savage crash at Charlotte in May of 1955. But even as he lay in the hospital with a concussion and broken leg, Thomas promised himself that not only would he be back, he would win before the season was out.

Thomas returned in early August, then posted a win at Raleigh on August 20. On Labor Day weekend, he won the big one: the Southern 500 at Darlington.

2. ROBERT "RED" BYRON

The injuries that sidelined Red Byron did not happen on a racetrack; they came during World War II.

Byron had made a name for himself long before NASCAR got off the ground, but like many other young men, he put his career on hold when war broke out in 1941. He enlisted in the Army Air Corps and successfully flew 57 missions. On the 58th, he was shot down over the Aleutian Islands. He spent more than two years in army hospitals while doctors tried to piece his shattered left leg back together.

Byron returned to racing with a special steel stirrup, which was attached to the clutch. He was better with one good leg than most men were with two.

When NASCAR raced its first official season in 1949, Byron was crowned the champion.

3. BOB FLOCK

The eldest of the three racing Flock brothers raced only part-time on NASCAR's Grand National circuit from 1949–1956, but Bob was a force every time he was on the track.

In the final race of the 1951 season at Mobile, Alabama, Flock took a tumble and had to be helped from his car. He drove 55 miles to Pensacola, Florida, before seeing a doctor. The doctor said Flock had fractured several ribs. A week later, still in pain, he sought a second opinion. This time, the doctor found the cause: a broken neck.

Against everyone's advice, he returned to racing on August 17, 1952, at Asheville-Weaverville Speedway in North Carolina and won the race.

Flock drove in only eight more Grand Nationals, but he had proven his point.

4. ERNIE IRVAN

On August 20, 1994, Ernie Irvan knocked on Death's door. Pounded on it. Death turned him away.

Irvan was going out for a Saturday morning practice for the Goodwrench 400 at Brooklyn, Michigan. Only a few laps into the session, Irvan's car veered head-on into the wall at 190 mph.

He suffered major injuries to his brain, lungs, and heart. He was given only a 10 percent chance to live, much less ever drive a race car again.

Irvan spent more than a year in rehabilitation but miraculously returned to Winston Cup racing on October 1, 1995, at North Wilkesboro, North Carolina. In 1996, he scored two wins, at Loudon, New Hampshire, and Richmond.

Michigan, however, continued to play a major role in his racing career. At the track that almost killed him, Irvan won the June race at Michigan in 1997, three years after his near-fatal crash.

Then, in August of 1999, almost five years to the day from his first accident, he was injured again—at Michigan. This time, he decided not to tempt fate anymore. Irvan retired.

5. NEIL BONNETT

Neil Bonnett, a popular member of racing's "Alabama Gang," suffered a severe concussion in the 1990 TranSouth 500 at Darlington that sidelined him for more than three years.

Bonnett eventually recovered from the amnesia that was the most serious effect of the wreck. He was gaining a reputation as one of the better race broadcasters around, but the lure of the cockpit proved too strong.

In 1993, Bonnett attempted a comeback at Talladega Superspeedway. In a frightening crash on lap 132, Bonnett's car became airborne and plowed into the steel wire fence on

Neil Bonnett

Bryant McMurray

Neil Bonnett, a Hueytown member of racing's "Alabama Gang," won 18 races in his career. He was killed in a crash during practice for the 1994 Daytona 500.

the homestrech. Bonnett was not injured and continued with his comeback.

In February of 1994, Bonnett was practicing for the season-opening Daytona 500 when his car hit the wall at full speed. This time, he did not survive.

6. **LEE PETTY**

The torch had already been passed when Lee Petty returned to racing on April 22, 1962, after his near-fatal crash in the 1960 Daytona 500. His son Richard was on his way to becoming NASCAR's all-time winningest driver, but the old man had to give it one more try.

Richard Petty won the Virginia 500 at Martinsville Speedway, but his father, with relief help from Jim Paschal, finished fifth.

It was the only race in which the elder Petty competed in 1962, and he would drive in only five more races after that.

He gave it a shot, but neither his heart nor his body was in it.

7. **JUNIOR JOHNSON**

Junior Johnson spent nearly a year in the federal prison in Chillicothe, Ohio, after being arrested at one of his family's Wilkes County, North Carolina, liquor stills in 1956.

Johnson's little "vacation" may have slowed his moonshining operation, but it did not dull his reflexes on a racetrack.

He had won five times in his sporadic appearances in NASCAR Grand National races since 1953, but when Johnson came back in 1958, he came back with a vengeance. He crashed in his first race, at Columbia, South Carolina, on April 10, but he was up to speed by the time he hit his old stomping grounds in North Wilkesboro.

Johnson took the lead on the 79th of 160 laps, then showed his tremendous talent. Driving too hard into the third turn, Johnson's car went over the dirt banking that served as a guardrail. He drove back onto the track without even losing the lead.

Johnson took three wins that year and would go on to a 50-win career that ended in 1966.

8. **FOnTY FLOCK**

Unflappable Fonty Flock made his "comeback" even before there was a NASCAR. Flock raced modifieds in the wild and woolly affairs on Daytona's Beach-road course in the 1930s and '40s before Bill France's idea of racing showroom stock cars had even germinated.

In the 1941 event, Flock and "Rapid Roy" Hall, a bootlegger from Georgia, tangled in the south turn. Flock's Ford landed upside down. Flock suffered a broken pelvis, a crushed chest, back injuries, and shock.

He sat out until the 1947 season, two full years before NASCAR was born. But when NASCAR was ready, so was Flock.

q. **MARVIn PAnCH**

Most race fans are familiar with the Cinderella story of Marvin Panch's rescue from a fiery crash before the 1963 Daytona 500; that is, they know that Panch told his car owners to put Tiny Lund in his car and that Lund won the race. They know what happened to Cinderella. They don't know what happened to the pumpkin.

Panch spent nearly four months in rehabilitation for his severe burns, then chose to make his comeback in NASCAR's most grueling race, the World 600 in Charlotte. Admitting that he was not at full strength, Panch still finished seventh.

His next six starts resulted in top-10 finishes, including three third places and one fourth. In September, he was runner-up in the Southern 500 at Darlington and in the following race at Martinsville, Virginia.

Then, on September 29, he completed his comeback in the Wilkes 250 at North Wilkesboro Speedway, out-driving Fred Lorenzen for the victory.

Panch's only complaint that day? His stomach was upset from some pills he'd taken for a head cold.

10. **CALE YARBOROUGH**

The doctors told Cale Yarborough after his crash in the 1969 season finale on December 7 at Texas International Speedway that when someone hits a wall as hard as he did, it's usually fatal. Then they told him it would be at least six months before he could race again.

They didn't know the man with whom they were dealing. Not only did Yarborough come back to win the pole for the Daytona 500 the next February, he did it with a record speed of 194.015 mph. Then he went out and won his 125-mile qualifying race, also at a record speed.

It would have been nice if Yarborough had gone on to win the Daytona 500, but he didn't. His engine blew after 31 laps. Life is sometimes good, but it's rarely perfect.

All in the Family

At one time, stock car racing was not exactly a whole-some family entertainment. Much of NASCAR's strength, however, lies in the continuity provided by the families who've been involved in the sport. Its tradition is largely built on a love for racing passed from father to son and shared among brothers. Here are 10 of the more notable families in NASCAR's half-century of history.

1. **THE FRANCES**

William Henry Getty "Big Bill" France came to the South from Washington, D.C., in the 1930s and built an empire around his love for auto racing. He brought order to the unruly bunch who drove race cars and weeded out shady promoters who held the sport back.

Big Bill fought off driver boycotts, the in-and-out support of American automakers, unions, and Congress; in short, he fought anybody who didn't share his vision, and he usually won.

In 1972, when he turned the reins of NASCAR over to his sons, William C. "Bill Jr." and Jim, they kicked it up a notch.

"Little Bill" took over as NASCAR's president and encouraged corporate America to come racing.

By making racing a viable advertising venue, Bill Jr. succeeded beyond what even his father would have imagined. The corporations that 20 years earlier had rebuffed his father became willing partners, and racing grew into a major-league sport. Multimillion-dollar racetracks replaced the dusty little "bullrings," and television networks spent millions more for the rights to show races.

When, at the end of the 2000 season, Bill France, Jr., announced his retirement and turned the presidency of NASCAR over to Mike Helton, a longtime employee, he made assurances that the Frances would be the power behind the throne. He installed himself as the chairman of a board of directors that included his brother Jim and his children, Brian and Lesa France Kennedy.

2. THE PETTYS

If the Frances are the first family of NASCAR, then the Pettys are certainly the second.

Lee Petty raced the family sedan—and wrecked it—in the first Strictly Stock race at Charlotte in 1949 and was one of racing's first superstars. He won two championships in the brawling early years of NASCAR and set the record for the most wins.

It was his son Richard who broke the record. Richard Petty went on to win 200 races—more than twice the number of his closest competitor—and seven Winston Cup championships. Richard's brother Maurice and his cousin Dale Inman turned the wrenches for most of those wins.

Richard Petty broke the mold. Before him, drivers were just that—men who cared little for publicity and wanted only

Bryant McMurray

Lee Petty

Until his son Richard broke his record, Lee Petty, the patriarch of
NASCAR's most famous family, had the most NASCAR wins with 55.

to drive race cars. Petty loved the fans. They loved him back. He became the model after which modern drivers pattern themselves.

Kyle Petty, Richard's son, took up the family trade. Though he will never match his father's total, Kyle has enough wins to make people know he's a Petty.

Adam Petty, Kyle's son, was being groomed to become the sport's first fourth-generation driver when he was tragically killed in an accident at New Hampshire International Speedway in the summer of 2000.

Though Richard Petty retired at the end of the 1992 season, Kyle still races. It's what Pettys do.

3. THE FLOCKS

The Flock family may not have had the stature of the France or Petty clan, but they were without a doubt NASCAR's wildest.

Carl, the oldest brother, raced power boats. Bob, Fonty, and Tim raced cars. So did sister Ethel. Reo, another sister, was a parachutist who made $50 a jump. Coretta, the tame one, was a barber.

It's about what you'd expect from a father who was a tightrope walker and bicycle racer in his youth and a mother called "Big Mama Flock" who kept the flock—no pun intended—together.

Bob and Fonty, older than Tim, hauled moonshine for an uncle in Atlanta in the 1930s and 1940s but discouraged their kid brother from the practice.

They couldn't keep him off a racetrack, however. Tim Flock won four races and his first Grand National championship in 1952. In 1955, he won a then-record 18 times and collected his second crown. He retired with 40 career victories.

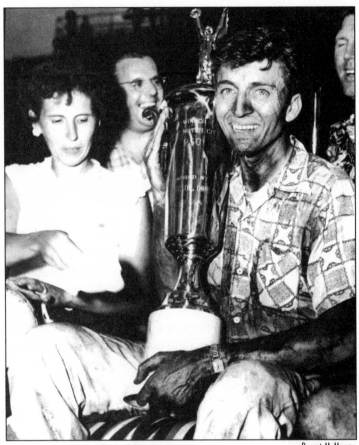

Bryant McMurray

Tim Flock

Tim Flock won the first of his two championships in 1952. Shown here in victory lane after the Detroit 250, Flock won eight races that season. Note that the drivers did not have "cool suits" in those days.

Bob Flock's career was cut short by an injury, but he had four GN wins. Fonty, who often raced wearing Bermuda shorts, won 19 times.

Ethel Flock Mobley never won a race, but she did finish ahead of Fonty and Bob in the second ever Strictly Stock race, on the beach-road course at Daytona in 1949. It was something she never let them live down.

4. THE EARNHARDTS

Ralph Earnhardt may have never won a Winston Cup championship, but his son certainly had the knack.

Dale Earnhardt followed in his dad's tracks, building his first race car from scraps that lay around the family shop. From the cast-off pieces that Ralph had used to win hundreds of races on the dirt and asphalt half-mile tracks all over the Southeast, Dale began a career that produced seven Winston Cup championships before his untimely death on February 18, 2001.

He also produced something else. In 2000, his son Kerry won an Automobile Racing Club of America race; that same year, Kerry's half-brother Dale Jr. won two races in his rookie season in Winston Cup.

5. THE ALLISONS

If there was ever a family tested beyond what a family ought to have to endure, it would be the Allisons.

Bobby Allison and his brother Donnie raced with distinction from the mid-1960s, with Donnie winning 10 races and Bobby 84 races and two championships.

Bobby's career ended in a savage crash at Long Pond, Pennsylvania, in 1988, and it was a harbinger of tragedy to come.

In 1992, Bobby's youngest son, Clifford, was killed during practice at a race in Michigan. The following year, Davey, his oldest son, was killed while trying to land a helicopter, his newest toy, in the infield at Talladega Superspeedway.

Clifford died before he could make a name for himself, but Davey had been on his way to superstardom. The slim, polite young man had recorded 19 wins in only six seasons at the time of his death.

6. **THE LABONTES**

Bob Labonte never rose to the top level of stock car racing, but he did something that not even the Pettys managed: He sired two Winston Cup champions.

Bobby Labonte was a kid who sneaked into his brother Terry's pits the day Terry won his first big-time race in the 1980 Southern 500. Bobby wasn't much older when Terry won his first championship in 1984.

By the time Terry Labonte won his second title in 1996, however, Bobby had arrived. When Terry locked up the championship by finishing fifth in the season-ending NAPA 500 in Atlanta, Bobby won the race.

In the 2000 season, Bobby gave his folks a third trophy for the mantelpiece, winning his own championship by an impressive 265 points over Dale Earnhardt.

7. **THE JARRETTS**

It is natural for a son to follow his father into the family business. The interesting thing about the Jarrett family is that the father, two-time Winston Cup champion Ned Jarrett, had two careers: racing and broadcasting. And his sons, Glenn and Dale, each followed one of his dad's career paths.

Before he was finished with driving, in 1966, Jarrett won two Grand National championships and earned 50 wins, which tied him with Junior Johnson for ninth on the all-time winners' list.

After he hung up his helmet, he went on to a successful career broadcasting racing on radio and television.

Glenn tried his hand at racing, with modest success, on NASCAR's AAA-level Busch Series before taking up the microphone.

Dale stayed on the track, moving from near-journeyman status to superstar when he began driving for Robert Yates's team in 1996. He won the Daytona 500 with Joe Gibbs's team in 1993—with his dad calling the race on CBS-TV—then broke through with seven wins for Yates in 1997.

In 1999, Dale Jarrett won the Winston Cup championship.

At the end of the 2000 season, Dale's son Jason was racing in the Busch Series with plans to move up to Winston Cup.

8. **THE BAKERS**

It didn't take Elzie Wylie "Buck" Baker long to figure out that, even in the 1940s, he could make a better living driving race cars than he could driving a bus.

Baker drove a Kaiser to an 11th place finish in the first Strictly Stock race in Charlotte on June 19, 1949, winning $50. Business would pick up considerably. Before he was through, he would win 46 races, 13th on the all-time list, and back-to-back Grand National championships in 1956 and 1957.

His son Buddy would follow him to greatness.

Buddy, a six-foot-five, 240-pound giant, scored 19 wins on the Winston Cup circuit, but perhaps his most notable achievement came at Alabama International Motor

Speedway on March 24, 1970. Driving a Dodge Daytona Charger, Baker completed a lap at 200.447 mph, the first time anyone had ever topped 200 mph on a closed course in a stock car.

Buddy's personal highlight, however, came on Labor Day weekend in 1970. He won the Southern 500 at Darlington, a race his father had won three times. Buddy still counts that as the apex of his career.

9. **THE BURTONS**

Ward and Jeff Burton, separated by six years, grew up racing on the short tracks near their South Boston, Virginia, home. Both made it to the Winston Cup level at the same time, in 1994, and Jeff won the Rookie of the Year title.

Ward won the first race, the A.C. Delco 400 at Rockingham, North Carolina, in 1995, but Jeff gained the upper hand. After signing with multiple-team owner Jack Roush in 1996, Jeff won 15 races through the 2000 season.

When Ward won the Mall.com 400 at Darlington in the spring of 2000 to get his second Winston Cup victory, someone asked him how it felt to finally get the upper hand on his sibling.

Ward replied, "You got a brother?"

10. **THE WALLACES**

Rusty Wallace came out of Missouri, the show-me state, with an attitude that said, "I'll show them."

Wallace had some success on the Midwestern ASA series before coming to Winston Cup in 1980, but he showed them in one race that he would be around for a while. Driving a car owned by racing magnate Roger Penske, Wallace finished second in the Atlanta 500 in his debut.

In 1989, driving for a team owned by drag racer Raymond Beadle, Wallace won six races and the championship. Through the 2000 season, now driving again for Penske, Wallace has recorded 53 wins and 35 poles.

Kenny Wallace, seven years Rusty's junior, has not enjoyed the on-track success that his brother has, but one would be hard-pressed to find a guy who enjoys his work more.

Kenny was the ASA Rookie of the Year in 1986 before he joined Rusty in North Carolina's hotbed of racing. In 1989 he was named the Busch Series Rookie of the Year and finished as the runner-up for the 1991 Busch Series championship.

His high-water marks through the 2000 season were a pair of runner-up finishes. He was second to Jeff Burton in the 1999 Jiffy Lube 300 at New Hampshire, and he followed Dale Earnhardt to the checkered flag at Talladega, finishing second in the 2000 Winston 500.

Mike Wallace, the middle brother, found success in several divisions before moving into Winston Cup full-time in 2001. He won four races in NASCAR's truck series, including the first truck race held at Daytona International Speedway, in 2000.

Good Sports

Race-car drivers are characterized as some of the fiercest competitors in sports, and they are. The atmosphere demands it. Nobody, however, said they couldn't be nice guys.

1. JOE WEATHERLY

The little pug-nosed driver from Virginia was as tough as they come, but he had a heart as big as his carburetor.

In a 25-lap modified race at Richmond in 1952, Weatherly and Sam DiRusso were going at it hot and heavy for the win. On the final lap, Weatherly hooked DiRusso's rear bumper, spun him out, and went on to take the checkered flag. DiRusso recovered to finish third.

Weatherly refused to go to victory lane, telling the officials that he had been too aggressive, and instructed them to give the win to DiRusso.

Weatherly happily accepted third-place money.

2. DAVE MARCIS

On June 6, 1982, at Pocono Raceway in Long Pond, Pennsylvania, Bobby Allison and Tim Richmond were battling for the win. Allison's car ran out of gas and stopped. Dave Marcis, who was not in the running for the win, slowed down and gave Allison a push back to the pits.

Allison managed to stay in the lead lap and eventually came back and passed Richmond for the win.

Then things got complicated. Richmond's team was owned by J. D. Stacy, who also sponsored Marcis's car. Richmond's team manager, Robert Harrington, blew a gasket, angered that a Stacy car would help an opponent beat another Stacy car.

Five days later, Marcis was informed that his sponsorship would be invalid after the July race in Michigan.

Marcis said that he would have done the same for anyone else.

"If we can't get along, we don't have anything," he said. "I feel like I'm being a gentleman to all drivers."

3. **RICHARD PETTY**

Richard Petty, as gracious as he was good, set an all-time record with his win in the 1967 Rebel 400 at Darlington. It was the 55th victory of his career. The record had been held by his father, two-time champion Lee Petty.

There was much pre-race hype about Petty beating his dad, but the 30-year-old driver said, "We've never even thought about it that way. As far as we're concerned, the Petty family has 109 wins."

4. **CARL KIEKHAFER**

If there was one man in racing whom the competition would never have expected to give them a break, it was Carl Kiekhafer. For Kiekhafer, racing was strictly a business whose sole purpose was to help him sell Mercury Outboard engines. He spent money lavishly on his teams (he owned several in 1955 and 1956) and went as far as he legally could to ensure that his drivers beat the pants off everyone else. But he did have a sense of fair play.

In those days, NASCAR had two unofficial divisions, one each on the East and West coasts, but both divisions were eligible for the Grand National championship.

Kiekhafer figured that if Tim Flock, his driver, could race at Syracuse, New York, on July 30, then fly in Kiekhafer's private plane to San Mateo, California, and race the next day, Flock would in effect gain a full race advantage over Buck Baker and Lee Petty.

But Kiekhafer didn't have the heart. When the plane left Syracuse, Flock, Baker, and Petty were aboard.

Flock won at both Syracuse and San Mateo, and in the California race they'd never have been able to afford on their own terms, Baker finished fifth and Petty sixth.

5. **RALPH EARNHARDT**

It's hard to imagine anyone with the last name of Earnhardt being a good loser, but Dale Earnhardt's dad played 'em straight up.

On November 11, 1956, at Hickory, North Carolina, Earnhardt, a hero on the Late Model circuit, got the chance to sit in the Grand National Ford normally driven by Fireball Roberts for one race, and he didn't waste the opportunity.

Speedy Thompson, who had been involved a few weeks earlier in a crash that seriously injured Herb Thomas, was roundly booed when he beat Earnhardt to the checkered flag.

Thinking that the crowd was upset over the order of finish, the officials ordered a re-check of the scorecards.

Thompson was still the winner, but Earnhardt, in order to quiet the mob, got on the public address microphone and told them he was satisfied with second place.

It was his first Grand National race.

6. JOE WEATHERLY, JUNIOR JOHNSON

In the summer of 1959, Ned Jarrett was in a tight spot. He had written a bad check on Friday afternoon for $2,000 to buy his first Grand National race car, a 1957 Ford, from Paul Spaulding. Jarrett figured, somewhat over-confidently, that he could win the $800 first-place money at Myrtle Beach on Friday and another $800 at Charlotte on Saturday, scrape up the remaining $400 when he got home, and beat the check to the bank on Monday morning.

He won at Myrtle Beach on August 1 but cut his hands so badly on the steering-wheel tape that he didn't last 50 laps at Charlotte the next day. Joe Weatherly, who did not have a ride that night, climbed in and kept the car in the hunt.

Then, under a caution flag, Junior Johnson relieved Weatherly and carried the car to victory lane. It was the same car Johnson had driven for two years when he drove for Spaulding.

Jarrett said that neither Johnson nor Weatherly took a nickel for their efforts, and he had himself a race car.

7. MARTY ROBBINS

Marty Robbins made a good living as a country-and-western singer in the 1960s and 1970s, and racing was his hobby. He did not have the money to run up front, but he loved racing back in the pack with the rest of the "independents."

But in the 1972 Winston 500 at Talladega, Robbins went a lot faster than he had ever gone, faster than even he expected to go. In the late stages, he was clocked at 188 mph, though he had qualified at only 177. He finished 18th in the race.

Afterwards, he asked NASCAR technical inspector Bill Gazaway to have a look at his carburetor. Someone had given him one that was a tad larger than it should have been.

Robbins refused the $250 bonus for being the highest-finishing rookie in the race, and NASCAR disqualified him for the illegal carburetor. The incident cost him more than $1,000. He didn't care.

"It was worth it," Robbins said. "In fact, I'd have paid that much money for a picture of Joe Frasson's face when I passed him."

8. "LITTLE JOE," AGAIN

Joe Weatherly and young Bob Burdick had a little bit of history between them. Back in February of 1959, Weatherly, running laps down, found himself in the middle of the photo-finish Daytona 500 won by Lee Petty over Johnny Beauchamp. Burdick said that Little Joe's "rough riding" had cost Beauchamp the victory.

At Darlington in the Southern 500 on Labor Day, Weatherly taught the kid a thing or two. When Weatherly's car fell out after 54 laps, Roy Burdick, Bob's father, asked Weatherly if he'd sit in for the kid, saying that the veteran could handle the rough track better.

Weatherly wound up finishing the race second to Jim Reed.

9. **DALE EARNHARDT**

Dale Earnhardt once pushed his buddy Rusty Wallace to a win. There was a long rain delay during the 1991 Miller Genuine Draft 500 at Pocono during which Wallace, who was leading the race, mentioned that he was low on fuel. No problem. Earnhardt said he'd give him a push.

When the race was restarted under the caution flag, Earnhardt, who was four laps down, nosed his Chevy up behind Wallace and Wallace switched his engine off for a couple of laps. Under NASCAR rules, the only lap in which this tactic isn't allowed is the last one.

Just before the green flag was to come back out, the rain started again. Earnhardt backed off, Wallace re-fired to run the final lap under his own power, and he won the curtailed event.

10. **FONTY FLOCK**

One thing about the Flock brothers: They looked out for each other. In a race at LeHi, Arkansas, on August 14, 1957, Tim Flock, driving one of Carl Kiekhafer's big Chryslers, blew by his brother Fonty for the lead early in the race. Tim had stretched the advantage to nearly half a lap on the 1.5-mile track when he ran out of gas.

Fonty pushed his little brother to his pit, went back out, and took over the lead himself. His good deed, however, nearly cost him the race. Speedy Thompson, who was running a lap down, was able to get back into the lead lap and challenge Fonty at the end but never caught him.

Tim Flock finished third.

First Time for Everything

Today it seems that we've seen everything under the sun in the world of NASCAR. There was a time, however, when everything was new. Below are ten stock car racing firsts.

1. FIRST NIGHT RACE

These days, when even massive Daytona International Speedway is lighted for night racing, race fans think nothing of it. Back in 1951, however, night races were a big deal. For one, Saturday night racing freed promoters from the restrictive "blue laws" against athletic events on Sundays. Second, racing somehow seemed to be more fun under the lights.

Frank Mundy, a one-time "thrill show" driver from Atlanta, beat Bill Blair by a lap at Columbia Speedway on June 16, 1951, in the first night race in NASCAR history.

Southland Speedway, a harrowing one-mile dirt track in Raleigh, staged the first lighted "superspeedway" race on September 19, 1953. Herb Thomas was the winner.

2. FIRST RACE IN THE RAIN

"Rain tires" have been tested with little success over the history of stock car racing, and as a result, NASCAR does not race in the rain. They did once, though.

Tim Flock, driving a 1956 Mercury owned by Bill Stroppe, took a win at the four-mile Road America road course in Elkhart Lake, Wisconsin, on August 12, 1956. Amazingly, his tires were not special; they were plain old street tires.

Not everyone handled the slick track as well as Flock. Hard charger Curtis Turner spun out and landed in a pile of hay bales. Turner reportedly had only one request: "Somebody bring me a pitchfork."

3. FIRST WIN ON FOREIGN SOIL

NASCAR has long billed itself as an All-American sport, but it has ventured beyond the borders of the United States.

Lewis Grier "Buddy" Shuman became the first driver to win a race staged outside the country on July 1, 1952. Shuman won a 200-lap Grand National points race at Stamford Park, a half-mile dirt track on the Ontario, Canada, side of Niagara Falls.

More recently, NASCAR has held exhibition races in Australia and Japan, but its only other points race on foreign soil came on July 18, 1958, when Lee Petty won a 100-lap race at Canadian National Exposition Speedway in Toronto.

4. FIRST FATALITY IN A NASCAR RACE

Rookie driver Larry Mann of Yonkers, New York, became the first driver fatality in NASCAR history when his Hudson Hornet overturned on lap 211 of a 250-lap race at Langhorne Speedway in Pennsylvania on September 14, 1952. Mann's car was painted green, a long-time taboo among racers.

5. **FIRST ROAD-COURSE RACE**

Al Keller won the International 100, a 100-lap event on a twisty two-mile track carved from the Linden, New Jersey, airport on June 13, 1954. He was driving a lightweight Jaguar.

It was the first and only NASCAR win ever posted by someone driving something other than an American-made sedan. It was also only the second time foreign cars were allowed in a NASCAR race.

The car was owned by bandleader Paul Whiteman.

6. **FIRST QUALIFYING RUN OVER 100 MPH**

If he'd had to turn, Tim Flock might not have made it. But qualifying for a race on the old beach-road course in Daytona Beach was done in "Flying Mile" style.

Drivers were allowed to back up a considerable distance to build up speed, and then their elapsed time over a measured mile on the beach side of the track was recorded.

On February 9, 1951, Flock flew through the timing lights in his heavy #91 Lincoln in 35.225 seconds, translating to a speed of 102.200 mph.

7. **FIRST QUALIFYING RUN OVER 200 MPH**

Benny Parsons recorded the first qualifying lap faster than 200 mph when he won the pole for the 1982 Winston 500 at Talladega. Parsons drove the Ranier Racing Pontiac to a lap at 200.176 mph.

(In March 1970 at Talladega, Buddy Baker, testing tires for Goodyear in Cotton Owens' Dodge, had become the first driver to break the 200 mph barrier.)

Parsons's luck didn't carry through the weekend. Darrell Waltrip pulled a nifty slingshot move to pass Parsons for the lead on the final lap of the race and drew Terry Labonte along with him. Parsons wound up third.

8. FIRST MILLION-DOLLAR PAYDAY

He was already "Awesome Bill From Dawsonville," but Georgian Bill Elliott stuck a number on them on Labor Day weekend at Darlington in 1985 like no one else in the history of stock car racing.

Elliott, by virtue of winning two of Winston Cup's "crown jewel" events—the Daytona 500 and Winston 500 at Talladega—came into the Southern 500 needing only one victory to lock up the "Winston Million" bonus. (He had faltered badly in the Coca-Cola 600 in May at Charlotte to finish 18th.)

Elliott dodged a couple of wrecks early, then scooted under Cale Yarborough when Yarborough blew a power steering line with 44 laps to go. When Elliott rolled into victory lane, he collected a $1-million bonus for winning three of the Big Four. At the time, it was the biggest check ever presented in the winner's circle.

9. FIRST FLAG-TO-FLAG SUPERSPEEDWAY WIN

It is one thing to lead every lap of a race on a short track. A good driver and car can get a lap ahead of the field and sometimes stay there all day. On a superspeedway—a track longer than a mile—such a feat is almost unheard of.

Glenn "Fireball" Roberts took the lead on the initial lap of a 250-mile race at the 1.4-mile Marchbanks Speedway in Hanford, California, on March 12, 1961, and never had cause to look back. He led from flag-to-flag, winning the race by two laps over Eddie Gray.

It was the first time in history a driver had led every lap on a big track, and the record went unmatched until Jeff Burton led every lap of the Dura Lube 300 at New Hampshire International Speedway on September 17, 2000.

10. FIRST DISQUALIFICATION

It was a harbinger of a half-century of struggle between the men who make the rules and the men who try to get around them: The driver who was flagged the winner of NASCAR's first Strictly Stock (now Winston Cup) race was disqualified.

On June 19, 1949, Glenn Dunnaway set the tone for generations of rule-benders when, after winning the inaugural 150-mile race at Charlotte Speedway, he was disqualified following the post-race inspection. Someone had "spread the springs" on Dunnaway's car, a practice common to bootleggers of the day, to give his car more stability.

He was NASCAR's first "DQ," but certainly not the last.

Ten Indy-Car Drivers Who Won Winston Cup Races

There was never much crossover between the elitist Indy-car drivers and the roughnecks on the NASCAR circuit. Donnie Allison and Cale Yarborough were among the early stock-car drivers to try open-wheel racing, but aside from Allison's being named rookie of the race in the Indy 500, the NASCAR drivers never had much success. Indy drivers who double-dipped over into NASCAR had a better time of it. Here are the top 10.

1. **A. J. FOYT**

Foyt could drive anything with wheels. His seven Indy-car championships and four Indianapolis 500 wins show only one side of his driving expertise. Foyt won nine poles and seven races on the NASCAR circuit, including the 1972 Daytona 500.

2. **DAN GURNEY**

When it came to the 2.62-mile road course at Riverside International Raceway, nobody was better than Gurney.

Between 1963 and 1966, Gurney won all four Riverside races. He skipped a year, then won his final Winston Cup race at Riverside, the Motor Trend 500, in 1968. He also won four poles, all at Riverside.

3. **MARIO AnDRETTI**

The Indy-car crowd often argues over who's the better driver, Andretti or Foyt, but as far as stock cars go, A. J. was the more prolific winner. Still, with his win in the 1967 Daytona 500 in a Holman-Moody Ford, Andretti proved he could drive "taxicabs," too.

4. **PARnELLI JOnES**

Jones, whose only official win in a Winston Cup race was the 1967 Motor Trend 500 at Riverside, also won a NASCAR "sweepstakes" race at Ascot Stadium in Los Angeles in 1959. The sweepstakes races were not counted as official Grand National (now Winston Cup) wins since they included cars from the Short Track division, Convertible division, and Grand National cars.

5. **MARK DOnOHUE**

Donohue, like most of the Indy-car drivers who dabbled in NASCAR, won his only Winston Cup race at Riverside, the 1973 Winston Western 500. He was driving a lightly regarded AMC Matador owned by Roger Penske, but he led 138 of the race's 191 laps.

6. **JOHnny RUTHERFORD**

These days, the 100-mile qualifying races for the Daytona 500 don't count as official points races, but back in the 1960s, they did, so Rutherford's win in one of two races that preceded the 1967 Daytona 500 went into the record books. It was the 24-year-old USAC driver's first race in a Grand National car.

7. **TOny STEWART**

See A. J. Foyt, above. Like Foyt, Stewart made his mark in open-wheel racing before moving to stock cars. The 1997 Indy Racing League champion, Stewart was the first USAC Triple Crown champion (meaning he won championships in Midget, Sprint Cars, and Silver Crown cars).

He made the transition to stock cars look easy. Stewart won the 1999 Rookie of the Year title along with two poles and three races. He topped that in the 2000 season, winning two poles and six races.

8. **CHUCK STEVENSON**

Stevenson, the 1952 Indy-car champion, won on the 2.5-mile dirt-road course at Willow Springs Speedway in Lancaster, California, on November 20, 1955. It was only his second start.

9. **JIM HURTUBISE**

Open-wheel veteran Hurtubise picked up a few tricks from his fellow NASCAR competitors. In only his 11th start on the Grand National circuit, he lapped the field in the 1966 Atlanta 500.

Long after the race was in the books, he admitted that he had carried a monkey wrench in his car. A secret device to lower the car had been installed, and each time the caution flag came out, Hurtubise would crank her down a notch to get lower into the wind, improving its aerodynamics.

He tossed the wrench out on his victory lap, and nobody suspected a thing.

Bryant McMurray

Tony Stewart

Rushville, Indiana, native Tony Stewart served notice he was on the scene when he won the outside pole for the 1999 Daytona 500—his first Winston Cup race. He won three races and two poles in his rookie season and easily won Rookie of the Year honors.

10. JOHNNY MANTZ

Mantz won only one Winston Cup race, but it was the biggest one. In the 1950 Southern 500, NASCAR's first 500-mile race on a superspeedway, Mantz drove a lightweight Plymouth when everyone else raced Cadillacs and Oldsmobiles. Mantz was using tires similar to ones he had used on the AAA Indy-car circuit. While the heavier cars were murder on their tires, Mantz's little Plymouth wasn't, and he wound up winning by nine laps.

Who's in Charge Here? Me.

It took a man with an iron will to corral the wild men who raced in the early days of NASCAR, but Bill France was more than equal to the task.

Sometimes making up the rules as he went along, France's unshakable belief that he was right brought order to a sport where there had been none.

His son Bill Junior picked up the gauntlet in 1972 and showed that he had his father's touch.

1. KEEPING "STOCK" IN STOCK CAR RACING

On December 11, 1955, France disqualified not only the winner of the race at West Palm Beach, but the second-place driver as well.

With the automakers becoming interested in the sport, France set out to keep the "stock" in stock car racing. Joe Weatherly's Ford was found to have a non-stock camshaft, and Jim Reed's Chevy had illegal valves. They were bumped to the bottom of the rack and Herb Thomas was elevated to victory lane.

Furthermore, France announced that in the future, rule breakers would not only lose their prize money, but they would also be stripped of all championship points earned up to that race.

2. "WITH OR WITHOUT YOU, WE'LL RACE."

After a horrifying crash in the 1955 Grand Prix race at Le Mans, France, killed more than 100 spectators, the advertising of high-performance cars came under fire from the American Automobile Association.

Bill France tried to appease the AAA by outlawing super-chargers and fuel injectors in NASCAR in 1957, and he further said that any use of race results in advertising would result in the loss of all manufacturer's points.

When a fan was gravely injured at Martinsville in May 1957, the automakers said they were disassociating themselves from racing. Within hours, France issued a statement that said, basically, racing would go on.

3. DIGGING DEEP TO SAVE HIS SPORT

After the auto manufacturers' pullout in 1957, France, struggling to keep his sport going, announced that he would guarantee at least $300 in "travel money" for each racer who showed up for a Grand National race.

The pledge cut deeply into France's profits, but it may have saved his sport.

4. CASH On THE BARREL HEAD

Before the Crown America International Stock Car Race at Riverside, California, in 1958, France realized that revenue from the sparse crowd wouldn't cover the $20,000 purse. He insisted that the purse be posted before the race started. He collected $16,570 from the gate receipts, then took a personal check from promoter Gelard "Al" Slonaker for $3,430 to cover the rest.

Then—and only then—was the race allowed to start.

5. IT'S *WINSTON* CUP

When Winston poured tons of money into racing in the 1972 season, France reciprocated by virtually eliminating advertising competition for the cigarette maker.

Invoking the new restrictions on television advertising, France stated that any cigarette and/or hard-liquor sponsor advertising on race cars be limited to 32 square inches—a 4x8-inch patch. The restriction effectively dissuaded any other cigarette maker from sponsoring a team.

Since Winston's name was not painted in huge letters on any of the cars—just on every available wall and building at every track—the letter if not the spirit of the law was upheld. And France's cash cow was protected.

6. TEMPERING JUSTICE WITH MERCY

Popular driver Bobby Isaac was leading the 1972 Winston 500 at Talladega when he was black-flagged with six laps to go. His car did not have a gas cap. Isaac ignored the black flag and raced on. Two laps from the finish, he was passed by David Pearson for the win.

Under NASCAR rules, Isaac's scorecard would have been pulled four laps after his refusal to heed the black flag, which would have dropped him well down in the finishing order.

Bill France, Jr., in his first season at the helm, tempered justice with mercy. Isaac was fined $1,500 but allowed to keep second place. France said NASCAR had the option of penalizing, fining, or suspending Isaac, but he thought the light punishment was appropriate for the infraction.

7. "WITH OR WITHOUT YOU, WE'LL RACE," II

The 1969 Talladega 500 at Bill France's brand-new Alabama International Motor Speedway started off on the wrong foot. First, the track was not ready. Second, neither Goodyear nor Firestone had come up with a tire capable of handling the 190-mph speeds that the 2.65-mile track allowed.

The drivers threatened to boycott. France said, go ahead, we'll race without you. When the "name" drivers took him up on it, France filled the field with no-names and drivers from the NASCAR Grand Touring division race held the day before.

The race came off without a hitch, and an unknown named Richard Brickhouse got the only Grand National win of his career. France told the 62,000 paying customers to hang onto their tickets; they would be good for the next race at Talladega or Daytona.

8. GREASIN' A FEW PALMS

Bill France, Sr., tried not to play favorites, but he took care of his own.

In the early 1970s, Danny "Chocolate" Myers, the son of driver Bobby Myers who was killed at Darlington, showed up with a buddy at Daytona who had a junky car, just trying to make one of the companion races to the Daytona 500. They didn't have two dimes to rub together.

France brought over a Ford factory rep and introduced him to Myers, saying that the guy had been a friend of his dad's. After the two shook hands, Myers looked in his fist and found $200.

They didn't win the race, but they did make it to the next one.

And his buddy? Turned out that it was Richard Childress, who owned later the teams that Dale Earnhardt drove to six of his seven Winston Cup championships.

q. MY WAY OR THE HIGHWAY

In 1961, France fought off the most serious challenge to his authority ever: unions.

Curtis Turner, struggling to get enough cash to finish building Charlotte Motor Speedway, negotiated with the Teamsters for a loan. In return, he agreed to attempt to organize the Grand National drivers into a union called the Federation of Professional Athletes.

When it came time to fish or cut bait, France told the drivers they had a choice: the FPA or NASCAR. Everyone but Turner and Tim Flock knuckled under, and France banned them both for life. He later reinstated them, but not before he had made his point. He was in charge.

10. NOTHING FISHY GOING ON

France sometimes went to great lengths to see that NASCAR's rules were enforced. After a race at Raleigh on July 4, 1956, car owner Carl Kiekhafer protested that the flywheel on opponent Fireball Roberts's winning car was too light.

There were no scales available at the track, so the flywheel was carted off to a local fish market, put on the scales, and found to be legal. Roberts kept the win.

They Called Him "The Intimidator"

When Dale Earnhardt was killed on the final lap of the 2001 Daytona 500, it sent shock waves through an entire sport. On a racetrack, everyone thought Earnhardt was invincible. He was not; however, one thing was for certain: When he was racing, he never asked for quarter nor gave it.

1. VALLEYDALE MEATS 500, BRISTOL, 1987

Rain was headed for Bristol Motor Speedway on April 12 shortly after the halfway mark of the Valleydale Meats 500 when race leader Sterling Marlin felt his car bumped from behind.

It was Dale Earnhardt, and he was headed to the front. He hooked Marlin's left rear bumper when he tried to pass on lap 252, sending Marlin crashing into the wall.

Earnhardt finished first, Marlin 24th.

"I'm the leader of the race," Marlin hotly protested. "He's supposed to pass me, not spin me out!"

Bryant McMurray

Dale Earnhardt

Dale Earnhardt displayed his trophy after taking the checkered flag in one of the Twin 125 Daytona qualifying races in 1992. After two decades of frustration in the big one, Earnhardt finally won the Daytona 500 in 1998.

2. **GABRIEL 400, MICHIGAN, 1979**

It didn't take Earnhardt long to let people know how serious he was when he strapped on his helmet. Just after the midway point of his rookie season in 1979, Earnhardt raised his opponents' hackles at Michigan International Speedway in the Gabriel 400.

Earnhardt had led only one lap on the wide two-mile track, but late in the race, he went for more. With a handful of laps left, he bolted down toward the apron going into the third turn and tried to pass the leaders all at once.

He didn't make it, and he nearly caused a wreck, but he didn't back off. After the race, Richard Petty took him aside and explained the facts of life.

Darrell Waltrip said, "I like the kid. But he over-drives his car. He almost took us all out in the fourth turn with five laps to go."

Earnhardt admitted he was at fault but didn't see why the other drivers were making such a fuss.

"We were going three or four abreast. I slid up into Neil [Bonnett]," he said.

3. **THE WINSTON, 1987**

Earnhardt not only gave a few shots, but he took a stiff lick, too. In The Winston all-star race at Charlotte in 1987, Bill Elliott dominated the first two segments of the three-part race, but on the final 10 laps, the rules went out the window.

Elliott and Geoff Bodine got into a minor scuffle at the start of the final 10-lap shootout that allowed Earnhardt to take the lead when Elliott and Earnhardt bumped as Bodine went spinning out of contention.

Elliott, in the outside lane, crowded Earnhardt down onto the grass along the front stretch, but Earnhardt didn't even lose the lead. Then, according to Elliott, Earnhardt waited for him in the backstretch and put him into the wall.

"Never touched him," Earnhardt said. Earnhardt won; Elliott finished 14th.

4. COCA-COLA 600, 1993

In the 1993 Coca-Cola 600 at Charlotte, Earnhardt was penalized for 1) rough driving, 2) speeding on pit road, and 3) for having too many men over the wall on a pit stop.

The lesson to be learned? Don't get the guy mad.

Earnhardt, needing a caution flag to get back into the lead lap after the last two of those three penalties, spun out Greg Sacks on the 327th of 400 laps to bring out the yellow.

In the winner's interview, Earnhardt explained, "I didn't hit him, *per se.* I was just kinda up *agin'* him."

Winner's interview? Of course. The one-lap penalty didn't hold Earnhardt up for long. He got that lap back when Rusty Wallace spun out on lap 350, then he passed Ernie Irvan to take the lead for good a dozen laps later. (Irvan, of course, said that Earnhardt roughed him up when he went around.)

5. GOODWRENCH 400, 1996

Bobby Hamilton and Earnhardt were each giving as good as they were getting in a nip-and-tuck battle in the late stages of the spring race at Rockingham when Earnhardt "gave" a little more.

Hamilton had a slight advantage coming out of the fourth turn on lap 345 (of 393), but he was on the outside. The two cars touched, and Hamilton slid up into the wall. He saved himself, but after scuffing up the right side of his car, he fell out of the hunt. Earnhardt won.

"I'm real disappointed Earnhardt didn't race me clean," Hamilton said between clinched teeth.

6. GOODY'S 500, 1995

Earnhardt got off easy during the 1995 Goody's 500 at Bristol Motor Speedway. He roughed up Rusty Wallace early in the race, then banged Terry Labonte in the rear just before the checkered flag. Labonte crashed but won.

Labonte wasn't angry, but only because he'd hung on for the win. If he hadn't, Earnhardt might have had his hands full with the quiet little Texan.

Wallace wasn't as subdued. Earnhardt was being interviewed by a television reporter when Wallace walked up and tossed his water bottle at him. That was the end of it. In the old days, though, it might have been "tire irons at two paces."

7. DAYTONA 500, 1991

Fans of the late Davey Allison still say Earnhardt drifted up into Allison with three laps to go in the Daytona 500 and spun him out. Earnhardt fans argue just as vociferously that Allison pinched Earnhardt off.

The fact is, when Ernie Irvan bolted past Earnhardt for the lead on a green-flag restart with six laps to go—and Allison jumped to second—something had to give. Allison and Earnhardt touched coming out of the second turn. Allison wound up in the wall, finishing 15th, and Earnhardt was damaged enough to drop to fifth.

Neither driver was happy, but Allison was not reluctant to point a finger: "Racing is a business where you have to use your head," he said. "I was using mine. Somebody else wasn't."

8. SOUTHERN 500, 1986

When gentleman Richard Petty takes a verbal jab at you, you must be doing something wrong.

Petty, probably NASCAR's most mild-mannered racer, took a poke at Earnhardt when Earnhardt knocked him out of the race after only six laps.

Petty said of Earnhardt: "His mind goes out of gear when he flips on the switch to turn on the motor."

Coming from The King, that was pretty harsh.

9. ATLANTA JOURNAL 500, 1980

Earnhardt was one season past his Rookie of the Year campaign and two races away from his first Winston Cup championship when he ruffled three-time champion Cale Yarborough's feathers in Atlanta.

Yarborough was contesting Neil Bonnett for the win, and Earnhardt was in third, challenging Yarborough to get back into the lead lap. He was also racing Yarborough for the championship.

The final three laps were pretty rough, according to Yarborough.

"That's the worst piece of driving I've ever seen in my career as a race-car driver," Yarborough said.

And Earnhardt? "I never touched him," he said.

10. FIRECRACKER 400, 1980

Bobby Allison should have included a thank-you to Earnhardt in his victory-lane remarks in the July Daytona race. In the opinion of second-place finisher David Pearson, Earnhardt handed the win to Allison.

Riding third, Earnhardt made a bold bid for the lead on the final lap, got trapped behind some slower cars, and forced second-place David Pearson nearly into the wall in the second turn. Pearson came back to nip Earnhardt for second place but couldn't catch Allison.

"I had to back off, and I knew I couldn't win after that," Pearson said.

Earnhardt admitted his mistake, simply saying he wanted to get by the lapped cars as soon as he could.

The Ever-Quotable
nASCAR

These days, when you listen to a driver in victory lane, you'd think he owed his very existence to his sponsors—it's one long string of thank-yous. But if you catch a race-car driver off guard, every now and then he says something quotable.

1. PETTY'S BLAZE OF GLORY

Even in the final race of his illustrious career, the 1992 Hooter's 500 in Atlanta, seven-time Winston Cup champion Richard Petty managed to keep his sense of humor.

Petty's car caught fire when he crashed on the 95th lap. Instead of bailing out, he drove down to the first turn, where the fire trucks were. Not that it did him much good.

"I think all them cats wanted was an autograph, because none of them brought a fire extinguisher," The King said, grinning. "I had to holler at them to bring one."

2. HOW ABOUT, "IN THE SUMMER, WHEN IT SIZZLES?"

Darrell Waltrip was headed for a million-dollar payday in the 1989 Southern 500 when he found the fourth-turn wall. Twice.

"We got a little behind, and I guess I was trying to make it up too quick," Waltrip said. "I brushed the wall once, and if that wasn't enough, I did it again a couple of laps later."

Seeing the Winston Million bonus disappear with the breeze, Waltrip still managed a couple of bars from a song he composed on the spot, sung to the tune of "I Love Paris."

"I love Darlington in the springtime, I love Darlington in the fall," Waltrip crooned. "I love Darlington in the winner's circle, but I hate Darlington in the wall."

3. CONGRESS, MAYBE; PRESIDENT, I DON'T THINK SO

Kyle Petty came as close to a Winston Cup championship as he'd ever come when he won the AC Delco 500 at North Carolina Motor Speedway in 1992. Petty closed to within 94 points of leader Bill Elliott with two races left.

Petty, however, was a realist.

"I still think all the planets would have to line up funny or something" he said. "Me winning the championship would be like Ross Perot winning the presidential election."

4. MONKEY TIME IN DAYTONA

When Dale Earnhardt was outrun by Dale Jarrett in the 1993 Daytona 500, he was philosophical about his loss.

"Big damn deal," Earnhardt said after coming up short in his 15th attempt to win NASCAR's biggest race. "We've lost this race about every way you can lose it. We've been out-gassed, out-tired, outrun and out-everythinged.... There's nothing left to do but come back and try again next year."

Actually, it took five years. When Earnhardt finally got to the press box after his win in the 1998 Daytona 500, he unzipped his uniform, pulled out a stuffed monkey, and tossed him across the room.

"Finally got that [expletive] off my back!" he said, grinning.

5. **TWO CAN PLAY AT THIS GAME**

Dale Jarrett was upset after he got caught up in a big wreck on the final lap of the Save Mart 300K at Sears Point Raceway in Sonoma, California in 1993.

Kyle Petty was the guy who'd hit Jarrett, but Petty said the only reason he did was because he was watching Dale Earnhardt blatantly jump the green flag on the one-lap trophy dash at the end of the race.

Jarrett was hot.

"If those guys want to race that way, so can I," he said. "We've got plenty of cars at the shop."

6. **"WHAT SAY, BOBBY?"**

Neil Bonnett suffered temporary amnesia after he wrecked at Darlington in April of 1990. His mentor and fellow "Alabama Gang" member Bobby Allison had suffered a more serious brain injury in a crash at Pocono two years earlier.

Fortunately, both men recovered. According to Bonnett, their convalescence did have its lighter moments.

"Bobby was the first guy who stopped by my house," Bonnett said. "We were sitting there on the couch. Between Bobby trying to say what he was thinking and me trying to remember what he was saying, it was a helluva conversation."

7. **HEY, NOBODY TOLD ME**

If there was a conspiracy afoot to let Richard Petty sit on the pole for his last race at Daytona in 1992, as was vaguely hinted by some of the more skeptical members of the press,

Sterling Marlin didn't get the word.

Petty, who was retiring at the end of the season, set the crowd aflame with his qualifying lap early in the time trials before the July 4 race. His speed held up for most of the qualifying session, but then Marlin came out and bumped Petty to the outside of the front row.

Instead of the customary cheers, Marlin was hooted by the crowd.

"It was definitely a different feeling to get booed after winning the pole. I've never had that happen before," Marlin said. "I'm going to an autograph session in a little while. I wonder if I need to take a security guard with me."

8. WHO DA MAN? I DA MAN.

Junior Johnson is a man of few words, but you'd better listen, because he knows what he's talking about.

When Darrell Waltrip, who was driving for Johnson's team, was on his way to his second straight 12-win season in 1982 and his second straight championship, a hard-hitting reporter came nosing around the Johnson camp.

In a voice tinged with sarcasm, the reporter suggested that ol' Junior—considering how fast his cars were running—must have made a lot of trips to Detroit to see those motor engineers.

"No," Johnson said, cool as can be. "They come to me."

9. SOMEONE TO WATCH OVER ME?

Richard Petty's last win came in 1984, and his last race was in 1992. When he announced his "Fan Appreciation Tour" before the 1992 season, Petty said that he finally figured it was time to quit.

"Not winning races, not finishing races, not doing the

Bryant McMurray

Junior Johnson

Junior Johnson, shown here at the 1976 Carolina 500 at
Rockingham, N. C., was one of the most successful team owners
in NASCAR history.

things I am capable of doing—all of it adds up," Petty said. "God might have given me 25 years of good luck and I might be trying to stretch it to 35.

"Maybe He's trying to tell me something, like, 'Hey, you'd better get out of this thing before something happens to you and I can't look out for you no more.'"

10. **GROUNDED**

When Bill France, Sr., opened his new 2.66-mile track at Talladega, Alabama in 1969, the track was fraught with problems, not the least of which was the fact that the speeds were too fast for the tires.

With the drivers threatening a boycott of the Talladega 500, France appealed to one of the ringleaders, LeeRoy Yarbrough, as a fellow aviator. He told Yarbrough that he should treat the race like bad weather; that is, slow down and fly around it.

Yarbrough answered: "Bill, when the storm is as bad as what we've got at this track, I don't even take off."

Drivers You Either Love or Hate

Race fans are among the most fanatical in sports, and, like most others, they have their favorites. That means that on any given Sunday, a race fan has 40-odd other drivers to dislike. Some they dislike more than others.

1. **DARRELL WALTRIP**

It is hard to believe that Darrell Waltrip was warmly received during the final few seasons of his long and illustrious Winston Cup career after having been so lustily booed when he began it.

As a brash youngster out of Owensboro, Kentucky, "DW" earned the enmity of the fans and the men he raced against in the 1970s by first telling them he was going to beat them, then doing it.

He tossed so many one-liners at the opposition that in 1977 Cale Yarborough nicknamed him "Jaws."

After a particularly vociferous round of catcalls and boos during the drivers' introductions at Charlotte in the early 1980s, Waltrip invited the whole crowd to "meet me in the parking lot at the Kmart."

Waltrip used his quick wit as well as his hard-driving style to keep his opponents off balance. In 1985, he psyched Bill Elliott out of a championship. Elliott won an astonishing 11 races to Waltrip's three that season, but Waltrip used a combination of sharp barbs and a strong finish to win the title. It did not endear him to Elliott's legions of fans.

It took a wreck to change the fans' minds about Waltrip. In The Winston all-star race at Charlotte in 1989, Rusty Wallace spun Waltrip out in the final handful of laps while racing for the lead. That was enough to make Wallace the one to hate, and, almost overnight, the boos for Waltrip stopped.

"I hope that boy chokes on that money," Waltrip said after the race. For years, Wallace did. And Waltrip went on to win the Most Popular Driver award (voted on by the fans) twice.

2. LEE PETTY

The patriarch of the most famous family in racing was NASCAR's most popular driver in 1953 and 1954, but not everyone loved him. Lee Petty was a driven competitor and really didn't seem to care whether he made friends or not, on the track or off.

Petty was not above using a fender or a bumper on anyone who got in his way, even his own son.

At Lakewood Speedway in 1959, Richard Petty was flagged the winner of the race, and his father protested. A check of the scorecards proved Lee right, and the win—which would have been Richard's first—went to his father.

Lee's behavior wasn't as terrible as it sounds. Lee was driving a 1959 model car and Richard a 1957. In those days, a winner driving a current-model automobile got a $400 bonus.

"We needed the extra money more than I needed the win," Richard said.

3. **DALE EARNHARDT**

Rarely has a dividing line been so clearly demarcated: Race fans loved Dale Earnhardt, or they detested him. The fact that his annual souvenir sales are double that of any other driver indicates that he had fans. The boos that greeted him when he was introduced before a race were a sign that he didn't have them all.

Why did one man provoke so much raw emotion? To his fans, Earnhardt was a blue-collar guy—he never graduated from high school—who made himself a millionaire by being a brave man in a sport for brave men. To those who didn't like him, he was a guy who bullied his way to the top and raced by his own set of rules.

Case in point: At the 1999 Goody's 500 in Bristol, Earnhardt wrecked popular Terry Labonte on the last lap and won the race. NASCAR officials called it a "racing incident" and let the win stand.

"I didn't mean to wreck him," Earnhardt said afterward. "I was just trying to rattle his cage."

To which Labonte responded, "Have you ever heard him say he meant to do it? He better tighten his belts."

One thing about Earnhardt: He never let criticism faze him.

"I don't care if they boo me or cheer me," he once said, "as long as they're making some noise."

4. **JEFF GORDON**

Why do people hate a handsome young man who races clean, goes to church, loves his wife, and, by all accounts, is good to kids and dogs?

Bryant McMurray

Terry Labonte

Terry Labonte, a two-time Winston Cup champion, might as well
have had a bull's-eye painted on his rear bumper in the 1999
Goody's 500 at Bristol, Tennessee. Seven-time champ Dale Earnhardt
nailed him on the final lap, costing him the victory.

Consider the numbers: Two, seven, 10, 10, 13, and seven. That's how many races Gordon won per year during his sensational romp through the Winston Cup Series from 1994–1999.

Gordon has his loyal fans, but they are far outnumbered by the fans of the drivers he beat over the years, and those fans let him know it.

"Isn't it odd?" remarked one newspaper reporter who knew both Gordon and Earnhardt well. "The people who don't know Jeff Gordon hate him, and the ones who know him love him. With Earnhardt, it's the other way around."

Gordon, incidentally, bemoans his cruel fate all the way to the bank. At the end of the 2000 season, he had earned $35 million in Winston Cup prize winnings.

5. **FRED LORENZEN**

"Fast Freddie" Lorenzen was not the first Yankee to come down South and start whipping the Sons of Dixie on the racetrack, but he was by far one of the most proficient.

When Lorenzen came south from the Chicago suburb of Elmhurst, Illinois, in the 1960s, he was many things his opponents were not. He had the blond good looks of a Greek god, was a nonstop talker (which endeared him to the press), and, boy, could he drive a race car.

When he beat the legendary Curtis Turner in a fender-banging duel in the 1961 Rebel 300 at Darlington, he became an overnight star and villain in one fell swoop. Turner's fans booed him. Other fans were glad to see someone finally beat a bully at his own game.

Lorenzen never raced a full season in NASCAR, competing in only 158 events between 1956 and 1972, but he won 26 races, 33 poles, and had 84 top-10 finishes. He retired after the 1967 season, complaining of ulcers, but returned to compete in 29 races (winning three) from 1970-72.

6. **RUSTY WALLACE**

If the wreck involving Rusty Wallace and Darrell Waltrip in the 1989 running of The Winston was a career-turner for Waltrip, it was no less so for Missouri-born Wallace.

Boos rained down on Wallace that day after he took the checkered flag and followed him for years.

When he won the championship in 1989, his vow was to win his fans back. He'd make any personal appearance, auto-graph signing, or supermarket opening that was required of a Winston Cup champion, he said, to shuck the villain's cloak.

By 1993, when he captured the National Motorsports Press Association's Driver of the Year award by winning 10 races, Wallace had made good on that promise.

7. **CURTIS TURNER**

Curtis Turner was NASCAR's original party animal, a guy who had made a few fortunes in the timber business (only to squander them) and who raced just for the hell of it. His cavalier attitude showed on the track.

His nickname was "Pops," and history is unclear whether he earned the name because "Pops" was what he called everyone else or because he "popped" nearly everyone who got close to him on a track. Turner enjoyed nothing more than a good sheet-metal-swapping session, and it didn't mat-ter if it was a foe or his sidekick, "Little Joe" Weatherly—Turner loved to mix it up.

He was one of racing's early superstars and rogues, all in one package.

After a particularly "interesting" race, one of his competitors came over to Turner, who was leaning against his passenger car. The guy was carrying a tire iron, intent on settling his hash. Turner reached into the glove compartment, withdrew a pistol, and asked the guy what he was doing with the lug wrench.

The fellow told him, "Just lookin' for a place to put it down, Pops. Just lookin' for a place to put it down."

8. **RICHARD PETTY**

Richard Petty is perhaps the most beloved man in racing, but he was not always universally adored. Back in the 1960s and '70s, when the fans were as loyal to a particular make of car as they were to a particular driver, Petty's romp through several seasons in Plymouths and Dodges did little to endear him to the folks who drove Fords, Chevys, or Pontiacs on the highway.

Then there was the deal with Bobby Allison. Petty and Allison engaged in one of the sport's most spirited rivalries during the early 1970s until they called an on-track truce late in the 1972 season.

Earlier that year, their scuffling peaked at North Wilkesboro. Following the slam-bang race that Petty won, noted motorsports journalist Bob Myers said, "Petty and Allison are NASCAR's answer to the Hatfields and McCoys."

Allison put him on the railing at North Wilkesboro and Petty commented, "If I had films of this, I could sue him for assault with intent to kill, or something close to that."

Allison responded, "He hit me so hard that it bent my fender in. When he did that, I just ran back into him."

9. ERNIE IRVAN

They didn't nickname Ernie Irvan "Swervin' Irvan" for nothing. The Modesto, California, renegade's hard-driving style antagonized his fellow drivers as much as it did race fans.

Even before he landed his first first-class ride with Larry McClure's team in the 1990 season, Irvan was being touted as the man who would challenge Dale Earnhardt as NASCAR's tough guy. It took Irvan two races to go from "tough" to "crazy."

Irvan spun out early in the spring race at Darlington and was running 10 laps down when he challenged race leader Ken Schrader. Irvan slipped, slid into Schrader, and set off a 13-car crash. Popular Neil Bonnett was severely injured in the wreck.

At Talladega in May, Irvan was already pegged as a bad boy and did little to disprove it, touching off another big wreck. By the time the circuit came back to Talladega that fall, he was in such hot water with his fellow drivers that he made a humiliating public apology to them before the race.

Irvan would carry the rough-driver tag for years until his own career was cut short by a crash during practice at Michigan Speedway in 1994. Given only a 10 percent chance of survival, Irvan returned to race 14 months later and even won three more races. But he retired for good in 1999 after a second serious crash at Michigan.

10. JUNIOR JOHNSON

If Junior Johnson showed up for a race in a Chevrolet, the Ford fans booed. When he switched to Ford, the Chevy fans felt betrayed. When he got into a Dodge, well, you get the picture.

Johnson was one of NASCAR's early legends, racing to 50 career wins from the mid-1950s through the mid-1960s. Whether he was a hero or villain depended largely on your perspective.

The solid citizens of that era held up his conviction for moonshining as an example of the rowdiness of a sport that decent folk didn't watch. The fans of other drivers thought Johnson played too rough.

One thing the fans never disputed, though, was that he was the hardest charger who ever lived. In a landmark article on stock car racing in 1965, "The Last American Hero Is Junior Johnson. Yes!," author Tom Wolfe noted:

"It was never a question of whether anybody was going to *outrun* Junior Johnson. It was just a question of whether he was going to win or his car break down ... God! Junior Johnson was like Robin Hood or Jesse James or Little David or something."

That, he was.

Landmark Races in NASCAR History

Through the 2000 NASCAR season, literally thousands of races have been run. Though each was important to the man who won it, some stand out above the rest. Listed below are 10 races that had a lasting impact on the sport.

1. JUNE 19, 1949, CHARLOTTE

Prior to this date, automobile racing in the United States—outside of Indianapolis—involved a collection of wild, undisciplined men (and women) driving jalopies and performing in front of small crowds. There were no consistent rules, no championships to be won, and unscrupulous promoters were as likely to abscond with the gate receipts as not.

"Big Bill" France, who had put together an organization he rather grandiosely called the National Association for Stock Car Auto Racing, would bring discipline to this unruly sport. He made sure that the contestants got paid, that the cheaters were punished, and that the fans got their money's worth.

The local favorite, Glenn Dunnaway, won but was disqualified. France put a Kansan named Jim Roper in the winner's circle. There were crashes enough to feed the audience's frenzy and dust and noise enough to let the locals know something was happening down at Charlotte Speedway.

For the man who put it all together, it was a full day's work, but at the end of that day, "NASCAR According to Bill France" was here to stay.

2. **SEPTEMBER 4, 1950, DARLINGTON**

In the 1930s, a young entrepreneur from the unlikely hamlet of Darlington watched the Indianapolis 500 and came away from that race with a dream. It took two decades, but Harold Brasington saw his dream come to fruition on Labor Day 1950.

Over a gin rummy game, Brasington talked some of his buddies into backing a racetrack that was unlike anything seen outside Indianapolis Motor Speedway. He built it half the size of Indy, but bigger than any other racetrack in the country. It was paved—something unheard of in those days.

Bill France, Sr., needed a showcase event for his fledgling NASCAR touring circus. Brasington needed a big enough race to put Darlington on the map. It was a most propitious and timely meeting of two dreamers.

Seventy-five cars entered the race; twenty-eight finished. When a Californian named Johnny Mantz drove a little light-weight Plymouth to victory in the first Southern 500, both France and Brasington knew they were onto something big.

3. **JULY 12, 1958, COLUMBIA**

In newspaper parlance, it's called "burying the lead," but how would they have known?

At the very end of a story titled "Bob Welborn First in Race" in the July 13, 1958, edition of *The State* newspaper, the reporter writes: "Lee Petty's son, Richard, driving in his first competitive race, finished sixth."

Since the race was in NASCAR's Convertible division, it was not regarded as the first "official" race of NASCAR's greatest star. That would come six days later in a Grand National race staged, oddly enough, in Toronto.

But if you ask Petty where his first start came, he says Columbia. If you ask him the site of his first win, he will tell you the same place, a year later. That race, too, was in the Convertible division, and does not count among his many victories. Until you ask him.

4. FEBRUARY 20, 1959, DAYTONA BEACH

If Brasington dreamed, France dreamed in Technicolor. His own idea of a racer's utopia was a track twice the size of Darlington, two and a half miles around, with banked turns five stories tall.

When his Daytona International Speedway was completed in 1959, it was everything France could have hoped for.

In Greg Fielden's *Forty Years of Stock Car Racing (Vol. 2)*, Jimmy Thompson, who drove in the first Daytona 500, puts it eloquently: "There have been other tracks that separated the men from the boys. This is the track that will separate the brave from the weak after the boys are gone."

Lee Petty, the patriarch of stock car racing's first family, won the first Daytona 500 in a photo finish that took three days to decipher. Racing had been kicked up another notch. A big one.

5. MAY 13, 1967, DARLINGTON

In 1967, Richard Petty set a record that will never be touched, winning 27 of 48 races he entered.

None of those wins stand taller than the Rebel 400 at Darlington. When Petty finished a lap ahead of the field, it was his 55th career victory, breaking the all-time record.

More significantly, it was his father's record he broke. In a sense, the victory marked the passing of a torch from NASCAR's first generation to its next.

6. **JANUARY 10, 1971, RIVERSIDE**

Little seemed to distinguish the 1971 Motor Trend 500 at Riverside International Raceway from a thousand other races, save one detail: It was the first "Winston Cup Grand National" race ever run.

At the end of the 1970 season, the automakers were involved in one of their infamous "pullouts" from racing. At the same time, the government was telling cigarette makers they couldn't advertise on television anymore.

Junior Johnson had approached tobacco giant R.J. Reynolds about sponsoring his race car. When he learned how much money Reynolds had to spend, he sent them to NASCAR.

In 1971, through its Winston brand, Reynolds announced it would sponsor a race called the Winston 500 at Talladega and a special points fund worth $100,000.

The following season would see bigger changes. As his last act before stepping down as NASCAR president, "Big Bill" France worked out a deal with Winston that would have far-reaching effects. The tour was cut in half, with races shorter than 250 miles being placed in another division.

The Winston Cup Series was born, and it flourished. In Winston's 30 years of involvement, the championship fund has grown from $100,000 to $10,000,000, the champion's share from $40,000 to $3,000,000.

7. **FEBRUARY 18, 1979, DAYTONA BEACH**

Much of the nation was locked in the grip of a late-winter storm on the day of the 1979 Daytona 500, but the sun shone on NASCAR.

CBS Television was broadcasting its first live flag-to-flag race, and with much of the country sitting in front of the TV, NASCAR delivered.

The race was as exciting as they come. Cale Yarborough and Donnie Allison engaged in a last-lap, fender-banging duel worthy of a Saturday night short-track feature—at 200 mph. As the two spun off into the dirt on the backstretch, Richard Petty pounced into the lead and took the win.

Then, as Petty was taking his cool-down lap, TV commentator Ken Squier shouted, "There's a fight!" and the cameras flicked to a Pier 6 brawl between Yarborough and both the Allison brothers, Donnie and Bobby.

Sixteen million viewers who had been on the edge of their seats for the last part of the race must have gone nuts. This, they thought, is real stuff. This I can watch.

8. **APRIL 1, 1979, BRISTOL**

Finishing second through fifth in the 1979 Southeastern 500 at Bristol International Raceway were, in order: Bobby Allison, Darrell Waltrip, Richard Petty, and Benny Parsons, men who would eventually account for a dozen Winston Cup championships among them.

Finishing first that day was a 28-year-old rawboned rookie from Kannapolis, North Carolina, who would add seven of his own.

Dale Earnhardt took his first Winston Cup win in his 16th start. He won Rookie of the Year honors that season and his first championship the next.

If the Petty family carried NASCAR through two metamorphoses, Earnhardt was the iron butterfly who emerged from the third. Combining his indomitable prowess on the racetrack with an uncanny business savvy that belied his lack of formal education, Earnhardt turned himself into an icon.

9. nOVEMBER 15, 1992, ATLAnTA

It was a race that had a little of everything. Three men went into the final contest of the season with legitimate shots at the Winston Cup championship.

Davey Allison, needing only to finish fifth to win his first title, was taken out of the mix when he got caught up in Ernie Irvan's crash on lap 254.

That left Bill Elliott and Alan Kulwicki. The popular Elliott and the darkhorse Kulwicki played chess at 130 mph. Kulwicki didn't have enough car to win the race, but he could win the championship by leading one more lap than Elliott. Running on fumes, Kulwicki stayed on the track until he'd led 103 laps. When he pitted, Elliott roared on to the win, but he'd led only 102 laps. Kulwicki won the title by 10 points, the closest championship battle in NASCAR history.

The race featured a couple of interesting sidebars, too. Richard Petty, NASCAR's all-time leading winner, closed out his career after 1,177 races. And a young driver from Pittsboro, Indiana, named Jeff Gordon drove in his first.

10. AUGUST 6, 1994, INDIAnAPOLIS

Country came to town for the inaugural Brickyard 400 at Indianapolis Motor Speedway, and the city folks loved it.

Up until then, it was easy to separate the two types of race fans in the United States: You either liked your race cars with fenders or without; rarely were you a fan of both.

NASCAR stormed the gates of open-wheel racing's most sacred citadel in 1994, bringing 300,000 camp followers with it. To the surprise of many doomsday prophets, the place did not fall down. But it did rock.

Jeff Gordon, a youngster who could have made a career in open-wheel or stock car racing, treated the crowd to a dramatic victory over Brett Bodine.

Of course, it didn't hurt that Gordon had grown up in Pittsboro, Indiana, virtually in the shadow of the speedway. Both sides took a measure of pride in Gordon's win, and Indy has had open arms for NASCAR ever since.

One-Race Wonders

In over a half-century of NASCAR racing, dozens of drivers have competed with only one afternoon in the sunshine to show for it. Perhaps fittingly, many of the one-shot winners won at Talladega Superspeedway, a huge track that minimizes the need for driving skill but places a high premium on guts. Here are ten of the most notable one-race winners:

1. LAKE SPEED

One would expect great things from a driver with a name like Lake Chambers Speed. But when the Mississippi native came to Darlington Raceway on March 27, 1988, for the TranSouth 500, he had exactly seven top-five finishes to show for nine years of toil.

On that day, Speed had two things going for him. One, he avoided a seven-car pileup on lap 16 that thinned the field. Two, he was riding on Hoosier tires. The race took place during the early rounds of the tire war between "David" (the Indiana Hoosier Tire Co.) and "Goliath" (Goodyear), and Hoosier had the upper hand.

Speed took the lead on lap 170 of 367 and gave it up only during routine pit stops. He won by 18.8 seconds. It was his lone victory, though he raced until 1997.

2. **RICHARD BRICKHOUSE**

Brickhouse was a struggling young driver on September 14, 1969, the day that Big Bill France opened his mega-speedway in Talladega, the 2.66-mile oval then called Alabama International Motor Speedway.

The track was not ready. The surface was too rough, shredding tires after only a few laps. Thirty-seven of the top drivers withdrew, but Brickhouse didn't.

Brickhouse passed Jim Vandiver for the lead with 11 laps to go and scored his only Winston Cup win in his 26th start. He raced no more after the 1969 season.

3. **RON BOUCHARD**

Bouchard was a hotshot modified driver from Fitchburg, Massachusetts, who came down South to go up against the big boys in stock car racing in 1981. Driving in only his 11th Winston Cup race, the Talladega 500 on August 2, he looked as if he might have something for them.

On the final lap, Bouchard dipped low coming through the dogleg-shaped front stretch and beat Darrell Waltrip and Terry Labonte to the flag by two feet.

Unfortunately, the win represented Bouchard's 15 minutes of fame. He raced until 1986 without another win.

4. **GREG SACKS**

Sacks may not have been the best driver in the field in the 1985 Pepsi Firecracker 400 at Daytona, but he did have the best car. Driving a research-and-development Chevrolet owned by Bill Gardner, Sacks outclassed the field, winning by 12 seconds over Bill Elliott.

Gary Nelson, who later became NASCAR's technical director, was the crew chief and later admitted that the car may not have met NASCAR specifications. The victory stood, however, and it would be the only one of Sacks' career.

The win may have been more costly to Gardner. Hall of Famer Bobby Allison, his regular driver, quit a few days later.

5. PHIL PARSONS

Parsons owes thanks to the massive size of Alabama International Motor Speedway for his one and only Winston Cup win. His Oldsmobile ran out of gas on the 49th of 188 laps, but due to the length of the track, he was able to coast back to his pit and get fuel without losing a lap.

With that break, he was able to join a three-car fight for the win. He beat Bobby Allison to the checkered flag by two-tenths of a second, with Geoff Bodine coming home a close third.

The win did not springboard Parsons to stardom. He raced only sporadically in Winston Cup between 1989 and 1993 before returning to NASCAR's AAA-level Busch Series.

6. DICK BROOKS

A last-minute substitute in a lightly regarded car winning a race? It doesn't just happen in Hollywood. In August 1983, Dick Brooks of Porterville, California, showed up at the Talladega 500 without a ride. Jimmy Crawford had a year-old Plymouth, but due to his inexperience on big tracks, NASCAR would not allow him to drive it at Talladega. A deal was struck on Thursday, and on Sunday afternoon, Brooks pulled off one of the most stunning upsets in stock car racing history.

Buddy Baker appeared to have the race won when smoke appeared from his Dodge with 13 laps to go. Brooks, just a little over a lap behind, made up his lap by beating Baker to the caution flag, then out-ran David Pearson to his only career win.

7. BOBBY HILLIN, JR.

Twenty-six drivers led at one stage or another of the 1986 Talladega 500, but Bobby Hillin, Jr., led the lap that counted: the last one.

The 22-year-old from Midland, Texas, became the youngest winner in Winston Cup history when he took the lead with nine laps to go and held off Tim Richmond and Rusty Wallace for the victory.

Hillin raced full-time and part-time on the Winston Cup trail for 10 more years but couldn't recapture the magic.

8. LENNIE POND

Lennie Pond was worried about keeping his job as he headed to Talladega in August 1978. His boss, Harry Ranier, was openly trying to land Darrell Waltrip, so Pond drove Lanier's Oldsmobile flat out and belly to the ground.

At the end of the then-fastest 500-mile race ever run in a stock car (174.700 mph average speed), Pond was in victory lane for the first and only time of his career. He blazed past Benny Parsons with five laps to go, weaving his way through debris from a crash just ahead of them, and held Parsons off by two car lengths.

The victory didn't save Pond's job, however. The next year, Ranier signed Buddy Baker.

9. JODY RIDLEY

Rookie Jody Ridley was not the happiest man in the garage the day he won the 1981 Mason-Dixon 500 at Dover, Delaware—his car owner was.

Virginia native Junie Donlavey, a Southern gentleman in the truest sense of the term, had raced in NASCAR since 1949 without a win. When Ridley took the checkered flag two seconds ahead of Bobby Allison, it marked Donlavey's first (and, through the 2000 season, only) Winston Cup win.

Ridley should have celebrated more. It turned out to be his only victory, too.

Wendell Scott
Wendell Scott was a black man in a sport dominated during the 1950s and 1960s by white, Southern males, but he hung in there. He took his only Grand National win at Jacksonville, Florida, in 1964. Through the 2000 season, he is still the only African American to win at NASCAR's top level.

Bryant McMurray

10. **WEnDELL SCOTT**

Scott was by no means a one-race wonder, but to date, he is the only African-American driver to win a race in NASCAR's top series.

Racing out of a backyard shop and with his sons as crewmen, Scott outran the field by two laps in the Jacksonville 100 on a half-mile dirt track on December 1, 1963.

Buck Baker was flagged the race winner, but Scott protested that he had passed Baker three times. A laborious check of the scorecards revealed that Scott had completed 202 laps, two more than anyone else.

Nearly all of the 5,000 spectators had left the track when he was officially named the winner. It was Scott's only Grand National win.

On Other Playing Fields

M ost race car drivers are just that: drivers. They are guys who have little interest in anything other than grease and burning rubber. But that's not the case with all drivers. Some have shown athletic prowess in other sports, too.

1. GLEN "FIREBALL" ROBERTS

One of NASCAR's early superstars, Roberts didn't earn his nickname on a racetrack. He picked up his moniker as a flamethrowing pitcher during his days in Florida's youth baseball leagues.

2. DARRELL WALTRIP

Before Waltrip gained a reputation as a hotshot driver, he was a hotshot athlete in high school. In his hometown of Owensboro, Kentucky, Waltrip played basketball and ran track for Daviess County High School and set a state record in the 880-yard dash that stood for several years.

3. DERRIKE COPE

Cope was perhaps the best baseball player ever to don a driver's uniform. He was an outstanding catcher in high school and played collegiate baseball at Whitman College in Walla Walla, Washington. He was a pro prospect before a blown knee forced him to take a "desk job."

4. DALE JARRETT

The son of two-time champion Ned Jarrett excelled in several sports at Newton-Conover High School in North Carolina, earning all-conference honors in football, basketball, and golf. His forte was golf; he was offered a college scholarship but turned it down to go racing.

5. CALE YARBOROUGH

Yarborough earned a reputation as a hard charger on the racetrack, but before his driving days, he was also a knock-down kind of guy on the gridiron. An all-state player at fullback and linebacker in the 1950s for Timmonsville High in South Carolina, Yarborough even played a turn for the semi-pro Sumter Generals after graduation. Oh, yes. He was also the state Golden Gloves boxing champion in the welter-weight class.

6. KYLE PETTY

Aside from being one of NASCAR's genuine flakes early in his racing career, Petty played quarterback for Randleman High School in North Carolina. In his senior year, Petty guided the team to the state semifinals. He was offered scholarships from a couple of big colleges but chose racing instead.

7. LARRY FRANK

Frank was not a man to be trifled with. Though his only Grand National win came in the 1962 Southern 500, Frank

Bryant McMurray

Cale Yarborough

Hall of Famer Cale Yarborough won 83 Winston Cup races, which places him fifth on the all-time win list. As a youth, Yarborough was a Golden Gloves boxing champion, skydiver, and semi-pro football player.

was a Golden Gloves champion boxer and a former Marine who played service football in the Far East.

8. STERLING MARLIN

Marlin was a football standout at Columbia High School in Tennessee, playing both linebacker and quarterback. He appeared in four bowl games and was the team captain. He also played basketball in high school.

9. JUNIOR JOHNSON

It shouldn't come as a surprise that Johnson was good at anything he tried, and baseball was no exception. Johnson was a hard-throwing left-hander who played on one of the many minor-league teams that dotted the state of North Carolina in the 1940s and 1950s.

Johnson doesn't brag on it much himself, but according to his friends, he was good enough to get a major-league tryout.

Unfortunately, he turned a tractor over on his farm and injured his arm before he could fulfill his baseball dream. Had things turned out differently, we might be putting Johnson's name up beside that of his close friend, former New York Yankee lefty Whitey Ford.

10. BUDDY BAKER

At 6-5, Buddy Baker was suited for tight end, but he became a standout tackle during his prep days at Garinger High School in Charlotte.

Outside the Lines

I n racing, sometimes the best action occurs off the track.

1. GEOFFREY BODINE

Geoffrey Bodine, an established modified driver from the Northeast, was still a novice on big tracks like Daytona International Speedway when he showed up for the 1981 Daytona 500.

In only his second race on the big oval, Bodine's Pontiac slipped coming out of turn 4 on lap 48 and skidded across the track into the infield.

He hit the dirt embankment that separated the track from the spectators with a good head of steam, jumped it, and slammed into a station wagon belonging to a local television station.

No one was hurt, although the spectators scattered like a covey of quail.

History does not record whether Bodine made the six o'clock news or not.

2. JOHnny ALLEn

Johnny Allen's thrilling win over Rex White at Bowman-Gray Stadium in Winston-Salem on June 16, 1962, went right down to the wire. And beyond.

Allen and White came barreling off the fourth turn headed for the checkered flag, neck-and-neck. Allen floored his accelerator so hard that he couldn't slow down in time to make the sharp first turn. Over the wall he went.

He won by six inches and tore up his Pontiac in less than a quarter of a lap.

3. LEE PETTY AnD JOHnny BEAUCHAMP

The two men who had battled down to the wire in the first Daytona 500 in 1959 would be the same two whose fates would be joined in disaster at the same track two years later.

On February 24, 1961, Lee Petty, who won the inaugural Daytona 500 in a photo-finish with Johnny Beauchamp, locked bumpers with Beauchamp 37 laps into the second 40-lap qualifying race.

At 150 miles per hour, both cars broke through the guardrail and sailed out over the five-story third turn. Beauchamp sustained head injuries, but Petty was the most severely hurt. He suffered a punctured lung, fractured left thigh, a broken collarbone, and multiple internal injuries. (A spectator, A. B. Kelly of Nashville, also lacerated his right hand while trying to assist Petty moments after the crash. The car rolled over onto his hand.)

The accident in effect ended Petty's career. He would drive in several races after that, but his heart was not in it.

Want more irony? Hours before, in the first qualifying race, Lee Petty's son Richard had scaled that same wall.

Richard Petty, however, suffered only abrasions of both eyes and a cut hand.

4. **CALE YARBOROUGH**

The man who would eventually win five Southern 500s was three years away from his first victory in the fall classic at Darlington Raceway on Labor Day of 1965. At the end of that afternoon, Yarborough might have well wondered if he'd ever win at Darlington.

Yarborough was battling Sam McQuagg for the lead 118 laps into the 364-lap race when the two banged together as they entered the first turn. Yarborough's Ford, on the inside, actually jumped over McQuagg's Ford, cleared the guardrail, and went tumbling. Yarborough flipped half a dozen times before coming to rest against a light pole in the parking lot. Miraculously, he didn't get a scratch.

Joe Whitlock, a reporter who regularly covered the races, was walking from the infield tunnel to the press box, outside the turn, just as Yarborough landed.

A few minutes later, he joined his colleagues in the press box and asked if they wanted to know what Cale had to say when he got out of the car.

Dozens of reporters snatched up their pencils and notepads only to hear a stream of profanities that not only would never make it into a family newspaper but would have been too colorful even for a dime novel.

Whitlock's colleagues put down their pens and resumed watching the race.

5. **TINY LUND**

DeWayne "Tiny" Lund was a giant of a man, six-foot-four and 275 pounds, but he was as gentle as a puppy unless you

DeWayne "Tiny" Lund   Bryant McMurray

DeWayne "Tiny" Lund, shown here after one of his three Grand National wins, was a gentle giant until you crossed him. After Lee Petty wrecked him in a race, he took on the whole Petty clan—father Lee, sons Richard and Maurice, cousin Dale Inman, and even Lee's wife, Elizabeth—in a post-race melee.

crossed him. Lee Petty made the mistake of doing so at a race one night at the fairgrounds in Greensboro, North Carolina, in the 1950s.

That night, Lund's beat-up old car was running hot, so he was limping around, trying to stay out of the way and last long enough to win enough money to get home when, WHAM! Petty nailed him. Tiny's car was not good enough to win the race, but it was good enough to get in Petty's way the rest of the night.

When the two drivers got to the pay window, located on the elevated stage, they exchanged "pleasantries." Petty whacked Tiny. Tiny cleared his head, then took off after

Petty. At the edge of the stage, Tiny booted Petty in the rear, then joined him on the ground.

Soon enough, Richard and Maurice, Lee Petty's boys, joined in the fray, along with cousin Dale Inman, but Tiny was giving as good as he was getting while they all rolled around in the dirt.

Then, WHAM! WHAM! WHAM! Tiny saw stars. Seems that Lee's wife, Elizabeth, and her pocketbook had joined the action. Tiny called a truce, flinging a couple of smaller men aside.

"I can't whip all of you damn Pettys," he said.

Buck Baker, a bit amused over the whole thing, noted that Tiny seemed to be doing a pretty fair job of it.

6. JOE FRASSON

The most interesting wreck associated with the 1975 World 600 at Charlotte occurred in the garage on the day before the race.

Joe Frasson, who had been struggling to make the fields all season, came up short once again. After failing to make the show in the last round of qualifying, Frasson went to his hauler, retrieved a slegehammer, and proceeded to destroy his #18 Pontiac, much to the amusement of about 100 photographers and news reporters.

"I want to publicly announce the retirement of the Pontiac," he said.

NASCAR was not amused. Frasson was fined $100 and suspended 15 days for his sheet-metal work.

7. ROBERT HIGGENBOTTOM

David Pearson, an ace on the superspeedways, made a big mess on the first lap of the Festival 250 at Atlanta

International Raceway when he spun out, but his mess paled in comparison to that of the clean-up crew.

The racers stacked up like cordwood behind the Spartanburg, South Carolina, driver when he lost the handle. A dozen cars wound up in varying degrees of disrepair, but only three were knocked out of the race.

Not so for Robert Higgenbottom. He was driving one of the wreckers that retrieved the disabled cars. In the process, he flipped the wrecker.

Higgenbottom was unhurt, just embarrassed.

8. CURTIS TURnER

Curtis Turner was noted for being hard on his equipment. On June 2, 1957, he was nearly as tough on the fans.

In a 200-lap convertible race at Asheville-Weaverville Speedway in North Carolina, Turner took the lead on the first lap and stayed there. On the 86th lap, he was driving hard off the fourth turn when his Ford blew the right front tire.

His car crashed through a picket fence on the front stretch, hit the dirt embankment separating the fans from the track, went up on its side, and skidded to a halt about a foot from the front row of the packed stands.

Miraculously, no one was hurt.

9. JUnIOR JOHnSOn

If the fans at Junior Johnson's home track in North Wilkesboro, North Carolina, thought he might be a bit rusty after he'd spent a year in the penitentiary for hauling moonshine, he had a surprise for them.

Johnson had barely cleared the gates of the federal prison in Chillicothe, Ohio, when he showed up at the track on May 18, 1958, for a race.

Johnson was leading by half a lap late in the race when he went too hard into the third turn. The track did not have a fence, only a dirt embankment, and Johnson flew over it.

He somehow managed not only to keep control during a thrilling sprint through the high weeds outside the track, but he also jumped the embankment, landed back on the track, and never lost the lead.

When he beat Marvin Panch to the checkered flag, a crowd of 6,000 locals went wild. The "Wilkes County Wild Man" was home.

10. **EARL BALMER**

Earl Balmer didn't win any friends among the press corps on September 5, 1966, in the Southern 500 at Darlington.

Driving four laps down to Richard Petty, Balmer got a nudge from the leader on the 189th lap as they entered the first turn. At Darlington, the press box was located outside the first turn. Balmer went up and over the guardrail, struck the lower tier of the open-air press box, and sent a hundred reporters scrambling for their lives.

Fortunately, no one was hurt. Fortunately for Balmer, the press vented their wrath at the track, not at the driver. After the race, track president Bob Colvin was presented with an angry petition for a new press box.

Until it was replaced by an enclosed box (somewhat farther back from the guardrail) several years later, the press facility at Darlington was known as "Balmer's Box."

Unbreakable Records

Records, they say, are meant to be broken. For the record holders listed below, drivers who hope to dethrone them have their hands full.

1. RICHARD PETTY

In 1967, Richard Petty set two records that will stand as long as cars have wheels.

There were 48 races run that season, and Petty won 27 of them. In fact, from his victory in the Myers Brothers Memorial on August 12 until the National 500 at Charlotte on October 15, he was unbeatable, winning 10 straight.

Since the Winston Cup Series schedule was trimmed in 1972 to include only "major" races, both these records remain untouchable.

2. RICHARD PETTY, AGAIN

Petty's records alone could fill an entire chapter. In addition to the season and consecutive win marks, he established two other standards that won't be challenged: Total wins and total races.

Bryant McMurray

Richard Petty

Seven-time Winston Cup champion Richard Petty straps on his familiar "Petty Blue" helmet at Talladega Superspeedway in 1984.

Petty's 200 career victories—nearly twice as many as his closest competitor—speak as much to longevity as to excellence. David Pearson (105 career wins) posted a winning percentage close to Petty's, but nobody toughed it out for more seasons than the seven-time champion.

Petty drove in 1,177 races over a career that spanned five decades, from 1958 through 1992. At the end of the 2000 season, Dave Marcis was the closest active driver to Petty's mark with 878 starts.

3. LARGEST FIELD

On Labor Day, 1951, 82 cars lined up three abreast for the start of the second annual Southern 500 at Darlington. To this day, NASCAR has never squeezed as many cars onto a track for a Winston Cup race. (Just for the record, there were only 24 running at the end.)

As a footnote, 97 cars started a NASCAR modified sportsman race on the beach-road course at Daytona in the 1950s.

4. HERMAN "THE TURTLE" BEAM

Herman Beam was nicknamed "The Turtle" for good reason. He rarely risked charging hard. But he did something no one—especially no one in his day—has ever equaled.

From April 30, 1961, through March 10, 1963, Beam finished every single race he entered, a streak of 84 consecutive checkered flags.

Considering that teams in that era rarely carried a parts inventory for track-side repairs—and considering that drivers raced more for wins than for Winston Cup points—Beam's accomplishment stands alone.

Of Beam's 194 career Grand National races from 1957–1963, he failed to finish only 11 times.

5. DICK HUTCHERSON

Dick Hutcherson was a champion in the International Motor Contest Association when he came to NASCAR as a "rookie" in 1965. He set two records that will likely never be touched.

Not only did Hutcherson finish second in the 1965 points standings, he also won nine races and nine poles during his first full season.

He did not win the Rookie of the Year award, however. Hutcherson had competed in four Grand National races in 1964, which, at that time, disqualified him for the honor.

6. FONTY FLOCK, JOHNNY MANTZ

Fonty Flock and Johnny Mantz share the honor of coming from farthest back in the field to win a race. Mantz started 43rd in the first Southern 500 at Darlington in 1950, drove a lightweight Plymouth, conserved his tires, and won NASCAR's first big race by nine laps.

Flock, forced to start 43rd in the 1953 Raleigh 300, zoomed to the front and won by two laps. Flock missed qualifying because of ignition problems but roared into the top 10 inside 20 laps. When he passed Hershel McGriff for the lead on lap 196, it was all over.

Since the fields of Winston Cup races are now limited to 43 starters, someone may one day tie the record.

7. BOBBY ISAAC

There may be better finishers in NASCAR history, but it would be difficult to find a better starter than Bobby Isaac.

In 1969, the Catawba, North Carolina, driver won the pole position for 20 of the 50 races in which he competed. His record has been approached (Richard Petty had 19 poles in 48 races in 1967) but has never been topped.

Incidentally, Isaac was not exactly chopped liver when it came to finishes that season, either. He won 17 races.

8. JOE WEATHERLY

Joe Weatherly may have been the most fun-loving guy in racing, but he was also one of its most determined competitors.

After "Little Joe" won the NASCAR championship in 1962, he found himself without a full-time ride for the next season, so he began bumming rides.

Car owner Bud Moore furnished a car for only the major races, and Weatherly drove Moore's car in 34 events. Then he hitched rides, often in inferior equipment, for the rest.

By the time he won the championship in the final race at Riverside, Weatherly had driven for nine different car owners in 1963. One of those teams was Petty Enterprises. The guy Weatherly beat for the championship? Richard Petty.

It was the only championship ever won by a driver who drove for so many different car owners.

9. NED JARRETT

It was not uncommon in the 1960s to win a race by several laps. Back then, the race cars were more like their showroom brethren and more prone to breakage. That fact played into Ned Jarrett's hands in the 1965 Southern 500.

Forty-four cars started the race, and only 15 finished. Most of the top cars were on the sidelines when Jarrett took the checkered flag. When Buck Baker rolled across the finish line to take second place, he was 14 *laps* behind.

The track measured 1.375 miles in those days, so Jarrett's winning margin was 19.25 miles. Distance-wise, that remains the widest margin of victory in NASCAR annals.

10. AND, FINALLY, RICHARD PETTY

Sorry. You can't get away from the guy. A sampling of his more untouchable records: Most wins from the pole (career, 61; season, 15, 1967); most years with at least one win from the pole (career, 16; season, 13, 1960–72); most wins at one track (15, Martinsville and North Wilkesboro).

What Might Have Been

The history of NASCAR is filled with drivers who stayed on too long, drivers who probably shouldn't have been there in the first place, and those who left too soon. Below are listed some promising drivers about whom we'll always wonder what might have been.

1. "FAST FREDDY" LORENZEN

In the 1960s, the "Golden Boy" from Elmhurst, Illinois, came south to make his fortune, made it, and went home. To this day, Lorenzen says he quit too early.

Fred Lorenzen came to NASCAR after winning USAC championships in 1958 and 1959. He struggled through the 1960 season before winning three races in 1961 and a pair in 1962. In 1963, he scored six wins and 23 top 10s in 29 starts.

He was equally adept at racing on NASCAR's short tracks and superspeedways, winning five races at Martinsville, four each at Atlanta and Charlotte, and two at Darlington. In 1964, he won eight of the 16 races he entered and finished 13th in NASCAR Winston Cup points despite not competing in 45 of the 61 races held that year.

Lorenzen was the first driver in NASCAR history to earn more than $100,000 in one season ($122,588 in 1963) and won the Most Popular Driver award in 1963 and 1965.

He cited ulcers as the reason he returned home after the 1965 season. He made a handful of starts in the early 1970s before retiring for good following the 1972 season.

2. SAM ARD

If Sam Ard had not had his career cut short by a head injury, there's no telling how high he might have risen. In just 92 races in NASCAR's AAA-level Busch Series, Ard set a standard that may never be matched.

From 1982–1984, the Pamplico, South Carolina, driver scored 22 victories and 24 pole positions—in 92 races! Ard finished among the top five a total of 67 times and posted top-10 finishes in all but 13 Busch races in which he competed.

Ard won 10 Busch Series races in 1983, including four in a row, a record that has never been matched.

In 1984, he was on his way to a second straight championship when he crashed hard at Rockingham in the next-to-last event of the season. Despite missing the final race, he won the title by 426 points, the second-largest winning margin in Busch history.

Ard made a modest attempt at a comeback but never won again.

3. DAVEY ALLISON

Davey Allison, the son of Winston Cup champion Bobby Allison, was marked for stardom. Unfortunately, Fate had him marked for something else.

His father's career was ended by a head injury suffered in a race in 1988, and his younger brother Clifford was killed during practice for a race in Michigan in 1992. One year later, Davey Allison would also be dead.

Allison was named NASCAR Winston Cup racing's Rookie of the Year in 1987 after winning two races and five pole positions. He was the first rookie to sit on the front row for the Daytona 500. He later won NASCAR's biggest race, in 1992, after finishing second to his father in 1988.

In his six-year career, Allison won 19 times and finished third in the running for the championship in 1991 and 1992.

On July 12, 1993, Allison piloted his newest toy, a helicopter, from his home in Hueytown, Alabama, to Talladega Superspeedway some 60 miles away in order to watch a friend practice. He crashed while attempting to land in the infield, and 16 hours later was dead of massive head injuries.

4. NED JARRETT

Ned Jarrett had seen too many of his friends killed, injured, or finishing their racing careers on a long downslide. He didn't want it to happen to him.

Though Jarrett raced in NASCAR's Grand National division (now Winston Cup) as early as 1953, he raced for only six full seasons (1960-1965). In that brief span, he captured 48 of his career 50 victories and two Grand National championships. Before that, he was a two-time Sportsman champion.

In 1964, Jarrett joined with young Bondy Long to form one of the most formidable Ford teams on the circuit. In 55 races, Jarrett won 14 and finished second seven times.

In 1965, Jarrett ran in 54 of the season's 55 events, won 13, finished second 13 times, and placed third 10 times. In the 1965 Southern 500, he won by a whopping 14 laps over the field, still the largest margin of victory, mile-wise, in NASCAR history.

Jarrett competed in 21 events in 1966, but after going winless, he hung up his helmet for good.

5. TIM RICHMOND

Tim Richmond was a flamboyant star who loved fast cars, fast women, and good times.

After being named the rookie of the race in the 1980 Indianapolis 500, he came to NASCAR and scored 13 wins and 14 poles in his brief (185 races) career.

In 1986, he won seven races and eight poles, more than any driver that season, and was named NASCAR's Driver of the Year along with Dale Earnhardt, his closest friend and closest rival.

Within a week after winning that award, he was diagnosed with AIDS.

Richmond came back to win two more races, then disappeared again. In his second comeback attempt, Richmond found himself battling NASCAR and the sport's establishment. Because of the public misunderstanding surrounding the disease, NASCAR demanded Richmond's medical records, and Richmond resisted. It was a fight as futile as his struggle against AIDS.

He died in a West Palm Beach, Florida, hospital on August 13, 1989, cut off and shut out from nearly everyone in racing. Richmond was 34.

6. PETE HAMILTON

Pete Hamilton hardly fit the image of a typical stock-car racer when he came to NASCAR in the late 1960s, but in his brief career, he would leave a lasting impression.

Hamilton, whose father was the dean of the business school at Northeast University in Boston, joined the rough-

and-tumble of NASCAR's Sportsman (now Busch Series) division in 1967 and at the age of 24 won the championship and 17 races.

In his freshman season at the top level, he scored six top-10 finishes in 16 starts, winning the 1968 Rookie of the Year title. In 1970, driving a Plymouth Superbird owned by Petty Enterprises, he scored a stunning upset in the Daytona 500. He passed three-time champion David Pearson with nine laps to go and held him off by half a second.

Hamilton competed in only 64 Grand National events from 1968–73 but recorded four wins, three poles, and 33 top 10s.

He won one race with owner Cotton Owens in 1971, but back injuries from an accident early in his career forced him into early retirement.

7. ALAN KULWICKI

Alan Kulwicki defied every convention in stock car racing to become a champion.

He was from the Midwest at a time when precious few non-Southerners were making it in NASCAR's Winston Cup division. He was a college graduate (mechanical engineering) in a sport where a degree was, at best, superfluous.

He came south in 1985 with literally everything he owned in one small trailer, then watched as it all burned to the ground.

In 1986, he scraped together enough money to make five races and won the Winston Cup Rookie of the Year title. His first win came in 1988 in Phoenix, prompting offers from several well-heeled team owners. Stubbornly independent, Kulwicki turned them all down. He was going to do it his way.

In 1992, he pulled off one of the most amazing upsets in racing history. Trailing by 278 points with six races remaining, Kulwicki stormed through the final half-dozen events to win the championship by 10 points over Bill Elliott and team owner Junior Johnson—a man who had reportedly offered Kulwicki $1 million to drive for him.

On April 1, 1993, just five months after he had beaten all the odds, Kulwicki lost his life in an airplane crash near Blountville, Tennessee. He was on his way to a race.

8. **LEEROY YARBROUGH**

When old-time fans speak of tragic figures in racing, LeeRoy Yarbrough is one of the first to come to mind. He blazed a path across NASCAR during the 1960s like few before or since, only to die in 1984 after a long bout with mental illness.

In 1969, Yarbrough proved that he belonged among the elite of the auto-racing world, winning seven races on NASCAR's Grand National circuit—and not just any seven races, at that.

Yarbrough swept both events at Daytona and Darlington (which included the Daytona 500 and Southern 500), won the World 600 at Charlotte, added a win at Rockingham, and got out of his sickbed to win the Dixie 500 in Atlanta with a 102-degree fever.

In the Daytona 500, he passed Charlie Glotzbach on the apron on the final lap to win; he won the World 600 by lapping the field twice. At the Southern 500, he passed David Pearson on the final lap.

In 1970, when Ford Motor Company scaled back its racing involvement, Yarbrough and his car owner, Junior Johnson, drifted apart. Yarbrough raced sporadically until 1972, then was not heard from again until February 13, 1980, when he tried to strangle his mother at their home in West Jacksonville. He was declared incompetent to stand trial and spent the remainder of his life in a nursing home.

9. MARSHALL TEAGUE

Daytona Beach native Marshall Teague won only seven times on NASCAR's Grand National circuit, but fans have to wonder what might have been.

Teague raced NASCAR modifieds in 1946 but was side-lined for a year in 1948 after a serious crash. When NASCAR began racing stock cars, he talked the Hudson Motor Car Co. into giving it a try, and the "Teaguemobiles," as his opponents often called them, became the dominant cars of the early days.

He switched alliances to the AAA, becoming its stock-car champion in 1952 and 1954, with the eventual goal of racing in the Indianapolis 500. He made the field at Indy several times, but his best showing would be a seventh-place finish in 1957. When he returned to Daytona in 1958, the day of the Hudson Hornet had passed and left Teague wondering if he had made the right move by leaving NASCAR.

In 1959, Bill France was promoting an Indy-car style race for his new 2.5-mile Daytona International Speedway in April. During the February Speedweeks, special days were set aside for the Indy cars to practice on the track in the hopes that someone would beat the world closed-course record established by Tony Bettenhausen's Monza 176.818-mph run.

Teague's car was not ready, but car owner Chapman Root, Jr., pulled out the Sumar Blue Special in which Teague had finished seventh at Indy. Teague ran it at 171.821 on February 7, but he felt there was more in the car. On

February 11, he ran a few warmup laps, then floored it. As he was entering the third turn, the front axle of the old car snapped, sending Teague into the wall.

When the rescue crew got there, they found Teague, 37, dead.

10. **BILLY WADE**

Billy Wade's star shone brilliantly in the NASCAR skies for two seasons, then was gone. Wade, from Houston, easily won the Rookie of the Year title in 1963 by taking 14 top-10 finishes in 31 starts.

In 1964, he moved to Bud Moore's team and became a contender for the championship. During the circuit's "Northern swing," he captured all four of his career victories, winning consecutive races at Old Bridge, New Jersey, Bridge-hampton, New York, Islip, New York, and Watkins Glen, becoming the first driver in NASCAR history to win four straight races. Those would be the only wins in his short career.

During a tire test at Daytona on January 5, 1965, Wade's Mercury experienced a tire failure, throwing him into the fourth-turn wall. The impact was fatal to the 35-year-old driver.

now, *That's* a Ballpark!

I f you've seen one basketball court or football field, you've seen them all, but racetracks vary widely. Some of the early tracks that played host to NASCAR races were limited only by the imagination and financing—or, more likely, the lack of financing—of their builders.

1. AUGUSTA INTERNATIONAL SPEEDWAY

If the drivers today dread going to the demanding road courses at Sears Point and Watkins Glen, they should have had a go at Augusta International Speedway in Georgia.

The course was three miles (compared, for instance, to Watkins Glen's 2.45 miles), and it had 21 turns compared to 11 at the Glen.

The track's first and only Grand National event was on November 17, 1963. The contest was slated for 510 miles but was cut to a mere five-hour race when qualifying times made it evident that they'd never finish 510 miles before a 5 p.m. Sunday curfew.

The field finished 417 miles, and Fireball Roberts was the winner.

2. SOLDIER FIELD

Soldier Field in Chicago, with its massive Roman columns, is better known as the home of "Da Bears," but it was also a hot spot for midget car races and, in 1956 and 1957, three NASCAR races.

On June 21, 1956, the Grand Nationals showed up for a 200-lap race around the one-half mile asphalt track laid out around the gridiron. Fireball Roberts was the winner.

A few weeks earlier, Chicago native "Tiger Tom" Pistone had taken a popular victory in a 200-lapper in NASCAR's Convertible division. Glen Wood won the final race at Soldier Field in 1957.

3. LANGHORNE SPEEDWAY

If your car handled through the turns, Langhorne Speedway was the place to race. The one-mile dirt track in Langhorne, Pennsylvania, which hosted NASCAR races from 1949–1957, was laid out in almost a perfect circle.

Next to Darlington, racers considered it the most difficult track because there were no straightaways on which a driver could catch his breath.

4. ONTARIO MOTOR SPEEDWAY

The massive track in Ontario, California, was too far ahead of its time.

Built in 1970, the 2.5-mile rectangular track was patterned after Indy, but its shape was not what made it special. Long before it became fashionable, Ontario sported elevators, restaurants, and suites for the use of corporations and well-heeled race fans.

Its first event, which was won by A. J. Foyt, had over 100 entries, and the field started three abreast.

Unfortunately, the track was situated on property that was more valuable for other commercial development. NASCAR raced there nine times between 1971 and 1980 (skipping 1972). The track went under the bulldozer about 10 years after it opened.

5. **OAKLAND STADIUM**

When the racers call a turn banked at 45 degrees "the flat corner," you get some idea that the track at Oakland, California, was not your everyday racecourse.

NASCAR raced there briefly in the early 1950s, and every trip was an adventure.

Compared to the 36-degree banking at Bristol (currently the steepest banking in Winston Cup racing), imagine what it must have been like to negotiate the 45-degree first and second turns, then plow into 60-degree turns at the other end of the Oakland track.

When NASCAR came to town in 1954, track officials tried to take some of the steepness out of the banking by piling dirt in the turns, making it possibly the only track in history to have paved straightaways and dirt turns.

Needless to say, the track underwent many alterations.

6. **LAKEWOOD SPEEDWAY**

Lakewood Speedway in Atlanta was a scary one-mile track on which NASCAR staged races from 1951–59. The track had the big-end, little-end feel of Darlington, with the added peril of a dirt surface.

What really made Lakewood scary, however, was its infield. The track was built around a lake that covered almost all of the infield. In its day, the water swallowed its share of out-of-control race cars.

The lake did serve a purpose, though. Carroll Tillman of Mableton, Georgia, crashed in practice before a modified race and his car caught fire. Tillman escaped unhurt and spectators helped put out the fire by pushing the car into the lake!

7. nORTH WILKESBORO SPEEDWAY

In addition to being the home track of one of the greatest racers in NASCAR history, Junior Johnson, North Wilkesboro's little .625-mile oval was unique in another respect: It wasn't flat.

Hewn from the foothills of the Great Smoky Mountains in western North Carolina, the track's backstretch ran uphill; the front stretch, downhill.

The track also had another feature that separated it from most Winston Cup tracks. Once you got in, you couldn't get out. There was no tunnel, only a crossover gate in the fourth turn, which meant that, unless you got in a wreck and left by ambulance, you weren't going anywhere until the race was over, even if you fell out in the early running.

8. MEMPHIS-ARKAnSAS SPEEDWAY

The largest dirt track employed by NASCAR was built on acreage in LeHi, Arkansas, once devoted to the cultivation of rice. It was a mile-and-a-half around and separated from the outside world by only a wooden guardrail. On one occasion, Lee Petty crashed through that railing and landed in a lake.

The track was host to only five Grand National races in the 1950s, and two fatalities occurred during the track's brief existence.

9. MARTInSVILLE SPEEDWAY

Today, the little half-mile track in Martinsville, Virginia, is one of the most picturesque on the Winston Cup circuit, but in its early years, it was not a place for the faint at heart.

Once fans got inside the high board fence, those who did not have reserved seats in the grandstands along the front stretch had the option of sitting or standing on the dirt embankment some five feet high just off the racing surface. In the turns. Where all the action was.

10. DAYTONA BEACH AND ROAD COURSE

Before Bill France built his high temple of speed, Daytona International Raceway, races in Daytona were staged on a 4.1-mile course that consisted of half pavement, half seashore.

Racers sped north with the Atlantic Ocean on their passenger side—or, depending upon the tides, sometimes *in* their passenger side—cut left along a rough passage through the sand dunes, flew breakneck down Highway A1A, then made another harrowing trip through the unpaved south turn before repeating the process.

The straightaways were fun; the turns were murder. The soft sand often caused cars to "hook a rut," sending them tumbling perilously close to the grandstands in either turn.

Of course, there was nothing quite like watching a driver "cross his car up," get sideways, and power-slide for half a mile before he entered the north turn, kicking up a rooster tail of sand and seawater.

Women Drivers

Despite a healthy number of women fans (some esti-mates say that more than 40 percent of the NASCAR audience is female), women have not had much success in racing. Here are ten of the more notable ones who have given it a shot:

1. SARA CHRISTIAN

Not every NASCAR race has had a female driver, but there was one in the first. Sara Christian, from Atlanta, started 13th in the first Strictly Stock race at Charlotte Speedway on June 19, 1949. With a little relief help from Fonty Flock, she fin-ished 14th.

Christian, whose husband Frank was a former racer and car builder, was enlisted by Bill France, Sr., to spice up his early shows. As it turned out, she could hold her own with the men.

In the pre-NASCAR era, Christian won six of 17 races before fracturing a couple of vertebrae in a crash in Atlanta.

She competed in six of the eight Strictly Stock races in 1949, and her best finish was a fifth place at Heidelberg

Speedway in Pittsburgh on October 2. A month earlier on the one-mile dirt circle of Langhorne Speedway, Christian finished sixth in a 200-mile race. For her efforts, she was invited to join winner Curtis Turner in victory lane.

2. **LOUISE SMITH**

To say that Louise Smith began as an untutored novice would be an understatement. Prior to her first race, she was instructed to stop if the red flag came out. Unfortunately, no one mentioned what she should do when she saw the checkered flag.

When the race ended and the other cars were returning to their pits, "Lou," as she was affectionately known, kept on rolling. Finally, someone remembered her pre-race "instructions," and the flagman brought her in—with the red flag.

Smith missed the first Strictly Stock race but showed up for the second one on July 10, 1949, on the beach-road course at Daytona. Unfortunately, she flipped her '47 Ford, but several policemen helped set the car upright, and she went on to finish 20th in the 28-car field.

From 1946–56, Smith won 38 races in several racing divisions.

3. **ETHEL FLOCK MOBLEY**

Ethel Mobley, a sister of the racing Flock brothers, made only one start in the new Strictly Stock division, but she made it count.

In the July beach-road race in 1949, Ethel drove a Cadillac convertible and finished 11th, ahead of such notables as Herb Thomas, Marshall Teague, Buck Baker, and Curtis Turner. It should be noted also that she finished ahead of two of her brothers, Bob and Fonty.

4. JANET GUTHRIE

Though best known as the first woman ever to compete in the Indianapolis 500, Janet Guthrie also tried her hand at NASCAR racing. In fact, she made the field for the World 600 in Charlotte before she did at Indy.

In 1976, Guthrie's bid to make the show at Indianapolis fell short, so she arranged to have a car available at Charlotte on Memorial Day weekend, and she did tolerably well. In a car that was owned by North Carolina banking executive Lynda Ferreri, Guthrie qualified 27th for the World 600 and finished 15th.

In 1977, she was the highest-finishing rookie in the Daytona 500 (12th), and she finished ninth in the Indianapolis 500 in 1978. In total, Guthrie had 33 Winston Cup starts.

5. PATTY MOISE

Patty Moise made her mark in NASCAR's AAA-level Busch Series. In 1986, her first season, she became the first woman to lead a Busch Series race. She made her debut at Road Atlanta, qualifying third, but lost her engine on the first lap.

Moise competed sporadically in the series in the 1980s and 1990s but raced two full seasons. She scored her best finish, seventh, at Talladega in 1995. She also set a track qualifying record in a second-round attempt.

In 1990, she married Busch driver Elton Sawyer and the two became the first husband-wife combination to compete against each other in a top NASCAR series.

6. SHAWNA ROBINSON

Shawna Robinson is another female driver to make her presence known in NASCAR.

In her NASCAR debut in 1988, Robinson finished third in the Florida 200 NASCAR Dash Series event at Daytona International Speedway. She also became the first woman to win a NASCAR Touring event, at new Asheville Speedway in 1988, and won her first Dash race. She was the Rookie of the Year that season and twice won the Most Popular Driver award before moving up to the Busch Series.

In Atlanta in 1994, Robinson became the first woman to win a Busch Series pole.

In the 2000 season, Robinson competed on the Automobile Racing Club of America circuit. In 2001, she was scheduled to attempt to qualify for seven Winston Cup races, with an eye to going full-time on the circuit in 2002.

7. JANET GUTHRIE, CHRISTINE BECKERS, AND LELLA LOMBARDI

These three women not only lent a feminine grace to the Firecracker 400 at Daytona in 1977, but they gave it an international flavor as well.

Belgian Christine Beckers and Italian Lella Lombardi joined American Janet Guthrie to become the first three women to start the same Winston Cup race since the first beach-road race at Daytona in 1949.

It was not a good day for the women. Guthrie's engine failed after 11 laps and she finished 40th in the 41-car field. Beckers lasted until lap 33, when her brakes went out, relegating her to 37th. Lombardi completed 103 laps before the rear end of her Chevy broke. She finished 31st.

8. ROBIN MCCALL

In 1982, car owner J. D. Stacy hired Robin McCall for three races. McCall was the 16th woman to become active in

NASCAR's highest division, but she was not successful in her first attempt.

McCall failed to make the field for the 1982 World 600 but competed in both races at Brooklyn, Michigan. Her best finish, 29th, came on June 20.

9. **MAMIE REYNOLDS**

Mamie Reynolds never turned a lap in competition, but she did have the distinction of being the youngest car owner on record and the youngest winning car owner.

The 19-year-old daughter of North Carolina senator Robert R. Reynolds bought a Holman-Moody Ford for the 1962 Southern 500. Darel Dieringer qualified 15th in the car but wrecked on lap 184 and finished 30th.

Undaunted, Reynolds ordered another car and Fred Lorenzen drove it to third- and 13th-place finishes before winning at Augusta Speedway on September 13, 1962.

10. **DOROTHY SHULL**

There was not a woman in the field for the inaugural Southern 500 at Darlington in 1950, but it was not for lack of effort.

Dorothy Shull, of West Columbia, South Carolina, spun her Olds three times in the second turn on the 15th and final day of qualifying and missed the show.

The Edge of Your Seat

"Thrilling" is a relative term. For one race fan, it's a daring pass in the dogleg at Talladega; for another, it's a 12-second pit stop that gives your favorite driver the lead. And then there are moments of brilliance on a racetrack that even a novice fan can appreciate.

1. BILL ELLIOTT, WINSTON 500, 1985

The Elliott brothers came to Alabama International Motor Speedway on May 5, 1985, loaded for bear. They got the bear, but not before shooting themselves in the foot.

Bill Elliott set a track record with his qualifying lap at 209.398 mph two days before the Winston 500. He was on a record-setting pace in the race when, on lap 48, smoke trailed from his #9 Thunderbird.

Brother Ernie diagnosed the problem as a broken oil fitting, but when Elliott returned to the track, he was nearly two full laps down. On most days, a race features a sufficient number of caution flags to help a driver make up lost laps, but on this day there was not one—until after Elliott didn't need it.

Elliott made up nearly five miles of lost position under the green flag, taking the lead from Cale Yarborough on lap 145 (of 188) and cruising to the win.

2. **MARSHALL TEAGUE, SOUTHERN 500, 1951**

Marshall Teague's Hudson was the fastest car in the field at Darlington, but since he didn't qualify on the first day, he started way back, 47th in the 82-car field.

Not a problem. In 12 laps, Teague passed 46 cars. It was—and still is—the most astonishing charge in stock car racing history.

It didn't last. Teague blew a tire on the 51st lap to fall behind, then crashed with fewer than 30 laps remaining. He finished 33rd.

3. **DALE EARNHARDT, WINSTON 500, 2000**

Dale Earnhardt boasted that he could see the air. After the Winston 500 on October 15 at Talladega, even the skeptics believed him.

Earnhardt did the impossible. He came from 18th to first in the last five laps and won the race.

In truth, Earnhardt came from 23rd in the final 15 laps after a caution flag bunched up the field. But he didn't start the remarkable charge until only five laps remained.

Hooking up with Kenny Wallace and Joe Nemechek in an aerodynamic "draft," Earnhardt pulled the three-car train right up through the middle of the pack, passing teammate Mike Skinner for the lead as he headed for the white flag.

When the threesome broke free of the pack, Earnhardt wove and danced his black #3 Chevrolet to break up the slipstream behind him and held off Wallace and Nemechek to the checkered flag.

"I personally won the race for him," Wallace said. "And he owes me."

4. **RICKY RUDD, NAPA 500, 1998**

Ricky Rudd's win in the NAPA 500 at Martinsville on September 27 was one of the gutsiest performances in auto-racing history.

Five laps into the 500-lap race, the cooling system in Rudd's Ford quit, forcing him to complete the race in intense heat. On several occasions, Rudd was tempted to turn the car over to someone else, but it was running too well not to drive it himself.

To make things worse, during one pit stop, Rudd told his crew to hose him down. The problem was, the hose had been sitting in the late-summer sun all day, and when it was turned on him, the water was near-scalding.

After the race, Rudd collapsed in victory lane, suffering from cramps, heat exhaustion, and second-degree burns on his back.

"It was like sitting on a hot iron," he said.

5. **LEEROY YARBROUGH, 1969**

Junior Johnson found a driver with a like mentality in a hard charger out of Jacksonville named LeeRoy Yarbrough. In 1969, Yarbrough would do what no one had done before: sweep NASCAR's Big Three races.

Yarbrough wiped out an 11-second lead by Charlie Glotzbach in the final 19 laps of the Daytona 500 to win it and finished two laps ahead of the field in the World 600 at Charlotte. But nowhere was Yarbrough's mettle more tested than in the 1969 Southern 500.

Bryant McMurray

Ricky Rudd

Ricky Rudd, shown here with the Robert Yates Racing #28 Ford, has what could be the most unbelievable streak in NASCAR history. For sixteen years, from 1982 to 1998, Rudd managed to win at least one race per season. Richard Petty topped it, winning in 17 straight years, but in most of those seasons Petty raced 40 or more times a year in contrast to Rudd's shorter modern-era schedules of less than 40 races per year.

Rain delays shortened the race from 500 to 316 miles. A showdown with the absolute master of Darlington, David Pearson, was set up on lap 200 when the final pit stops were made.

Reversing the strategy that had won the Daytona 500, Johnson opted for a harder compound tire than Pearson, that being an option in those days. With 30 laps to go, Pearson bolted into the lead on the softer, less durable tires and was running away with it.

Yarbrough chased a slipping Pearson down and passed him on the final lap when Pearson slapped the wall in the third turn. It was great theater; it was great racing.

6. JOHNNY MANTZ, SOUTHERN 500, 1950

The sellout crowd for NASCAR's first big race didn't know what to expect that sultry Labor Day at Darlington in 1950. No one even knew if stock cars were capable of racing wide-open for 500 miles. They certainly didn't expect the winner to be driving an "errand car."

Bill France, Sr., NASCAR flagman Alvin Hawkins, and mechanic Hubert Westmoreland purchased a little '50 Plymouth in the weeks leading up to the race, and France used it to run errands around Darlington.

Californian Johnny "Mad Man" Mantz suggested they run it in the race. After they quit laughing—even they suspected the lightweight car wouldn't stand a chance against the big Hudsons, Oldsmobiles, and Cadillacs—they let Westmoreland tune it up, anyway.

Mantz was the absolute slowest qualifier in the field, but he had a trick up his sleeve. He hustled up some of the hard-compound truck tires he'd used in his open-wheel racing ventures and quite literally ran the wheels off the rest of the field.

As the big cars ground up tire after tire, Mantz tootled merrily along at about 70 mph. At the end of the day, he was leading by nine laps.

He hadn't outrun them. He'd out-thought them.

7. **TIM FLOCK, 1952**

Tim Flock brought the crowd to its feet when he locked up the 1952 Grand National championship in the final race of the season at West Palm Beach. And he went to considerable trouble to do it.

Fortunately, Flock had only to start the race to edge out Herb Thomas for the title, because if he'd had to win it by his performance, he'd never have made it.

On the 164th lap of the 200-lap race, Flock's Hudson took a tumble, rolling over several times in front of the stunned crowd. He climbed out without a scratch, acknowledged their cheers, and said, "I bet I'm the only driver who has won a championship on his head."

8. **BUCK BAKER, nORTH WILKESBORO, 1955**

It was as close to seeing a whole day's work shot in the last split second as Buck Baker ever wanted to see.

Baker, driving a '54 Olds, took the lead from the outside pole on the first lap of a 160-lap race at North Wilkesboro Speedway on April 3. He led every lap, but just barely.

Dick Rathmann, driving a '54 Hudson, closed the gap in the final laps but came up three feet short at the checkered flag. At the time, it was the closest finish in NASCAR history.

9. **PAUL GOLDSMITH, DAYTOnA BEACH-ROAD COURSE, 1958**

It was the final run on the beach, and Paul Goldsmith gave Curtis Turner a run for his money. Bill France's new speed palace, called Daytona International Speedway, about four miles inland, would be ready for the 1959 season, and every driver in the field wanted to win the last race on the famous beach-road course. Goldsmith wanted it a little more than anyone else.

Using the Atlantic Ocean and Johnny Allen's Plymouth as picks, Goldsmith passed Turner with nine laps to go and took a 10-second lead. He'd blow most of that on the final lap.

His windshield wipers long since having quit, "Goldy" failed to see the north turn and went several hundred yards up the beach before he realized his mistake.

Goldsmith threw his Pontiac into a 180-degree bootlegger turn, and raced back to the track, beating Turner to the flag by five car lengths.

10. **FRED LORENZEN, REBEL 300, 1961**

It was Fred Lorenzen's first big win. It is still the one he claims was his best.

The 1961 Rebel 300 came down to a two-man show featuring the new kid on the block, Lorenzen, and the old master, Curtis Turner.

Lorenzen's crew chief and mentor, Ralph Moody, warned him that the old man would do anything to win. Anything. So Lorenzen set Turner up.

As the race wound down with Turner in the lead, Lorenzen kept testing him on the high side, testing, testing.

Then with two to go, Lorenzen faked high, and when Turner moved to block, Lorenzen dove almost to the apron of the track and scraped by before Turner could wreck him.

Lorenzen wept openly in victory lane, something drivers didn't do in those days. The emotion of beating his idol was just too much for him to handle.

Bryant McMurray

Glenn "Fireball" Roberts

Glenn "Fireball" Roberts was perhaps
NASCAR's first superstar. He was thoughtful,
eloquent (something rare in his era), and
could drive the wheels off a race car. His
career ended tragically when he died after a
crash in the 1964 World 600 at Charlotte.

They Died with Their Boots On

Ernest Hemingway once said that the only true sports are bullfighting, mountain climbing, and auto racing, because in no other "games" does the real possibility of death enter into the equation.

1. GLENN "FIREBALL" ROBERTS, 1964

Glenn "Fireball" Roberts was perhaps NASCAR's first true superstar, equally at home on the dusty half-mile dirt tracks that gave birth to the sport as he was on the fast, dangerous superspeedways that would lift racing to its next level.

Roberts died of burns received in an accident during the 1964 World 600 at Charlotte. Attempting to miss the spinning cars of Junior Johnson and Ned Jarrett, Roberts's car slid backward into the concrete wall. His fuel tank exploded on impact, and his car flipped and burned.

Jarrett jumped out of his own flaming car and helped Roberts to free himself, but it was too late.

When Roberts eventually succumbed to his injuries on July 2, 1964, Charlotte newspaper columnist Max Muhleman wrote that "it was like awaking to find a mountain suddenly gone."

2. **JIMMY PARDUE, 1964**

During the 1964 season, speeds had risen to such an alarming extent that something had to be done. One possible solution lay in making the tires safer. That required testing, and 33-year-old Jimmy Pardue was one of the 17 drivers who took on the task.

During tests at Charlotte Motor Speedway on September 22, Pardue was scheduled for a 10-lap run. On the seventh lap, a tire exploded as he entered the third turn. At 149 mph, four miles per hour faster than the track record, Pardue's bright red Plymouth crashed through the guardrail in the third turn, plunged down the 75-foot embankment, and dived into a chain-link fence 150 yards away.

Pardue died of massive brain damage and a crushed chest. It was conjectured that a steel fence post came through the windshield and struck Pardue in the head.

3. **JOE WEATHERLY, 1964**

"Little Joe" Weatherly, the 41-year-old "Clown Prince of Racing" from Norfolk, Virginia, was considering retirement after the season when he went to Riverside International Raceway for the Motor Trend 500 on January 19, 1964.

Weatherly's car was off the pace early and, after an extensive pit stop, he returned to the track with no hope of winning or even finishing well. His Mercury wobbled through the "esses" and hit the retaining wall solidly. Weatherly was one of the few drivers who disdained a shoulder harness, and his head allegedly hit the wall. He was killed instantly.

4. **ALFRED "SPEEDY" THOMPSON, 1972**

"Speedy" Thompson was one of the drivers who successfully made the transition from the short-track era to the super-speedways, but he was more comfortable driving the little dirt "bullrings" near his Monroe, North Carolina, home.

By 1972, he made occasional visits to NASCAR's Grand National division, but he died at Charlotte Fairgrounds, a half-mile track that supported weekly races.

On April 2, Thompson was driving a sportsman car in the main event when a caution flag signaled all the cars to a halt. He went to his pit, complaining of a shortness of breath. When the cars pulled back out onto the track for the re-start, he made only three-fourths of a lap before his car veered into the wall.

Thompson was dead of a heart attack, one day before his 46th birthday.

5. **BILLY WADE, 1965**

NASCAR was still in a state of shock over the deaths of three drivers in the 1964 season, and the prospect of another year of racing with inadequate tires was a scary one.

In January, Richard Petty and Houston driver Billy Wade, the 1963 Rookie of the Year and a four-time winner in '64, were conducting tire tests at the super-fast Daytona International Speedway.

Wade's car blew a tire as he entered the first turn and he hit the outside retaining wall, slid down the banking and back up it again, striking the wall a second time. When rescue personnel reached the car, the 34-year-old Wade was already dead.

6. JOHN DELPHUS "J. D." MCDUFFIE, 1991

J. D. McDuffie never won a Winston Cup race, but he got more joy out of the sport than many more-successful drivers ever will.

One of the last true "independents," he raced with inferior equipment and slim hopes of ever winning a race.

On August 11, 1991, McDuffie, a regular on the circuit since 1963, died instantly when his Pontiac crashed during the Bud at the Glen on the road course at Watkins Glen.

The race was only five laps old when McDuffie, 52, lost a tire and bumped into Jimmy Means. Both cars left the track and McDuffie's hit the tire barrier, flipping over Means's car.

Since he never slowed, it was speculated his brakes failed.

7. BOBBY MYERS, 1957

Bobby Myers was one of two brothers who died on a race-track.

On September 2, 1957, Myers, a 33-year-old native of Winston-Salem, was driving in the Southern 500 at Darlington when he crashed head-on into the disabled car driven by Fonty Flock. Paul Goldsmith also hit Flock.

Myers's car flipped several times before coming to rest in the third turn. He was pronounced dead on arrival at a local hospital.

8. BILLY MYERS, 1958

Less than a year after his kid brother was killed at Darlington, Billy Myers was leading a modified sportsman race at Bowman Gray Stadium in Winston-Salem when he suddenly slowed and pulled off the track.

Workers discovered Myers dead of a heart attack.

One of the most prestigious awards in stock car racing, the Myers Brothers Award, is named for the two men.

9. **MICHAEL RITCH, 1990**

Michael Ritch, a 32-year-old pit crewman on Bill Elliott's Ford team, was killed in an accident on pit road on the 296th lap of the Atlanta Journal 500 on November 18, 1990.

Ritch, a tire changer, was crushed between Elliott's and Ricky Rudd's cars when Rudd spun as he entered his own pit. Ritch died two hours later in an Atlanta hospital.

His death did have one positive effect—the institution of a speed limit on pit road.

10. **DALE EARNHARDT, 2001**

Dale Earnhardt died on the final lap of the Daytona 500 on February 18, 2001, doing what he loved: racing.

Earnhardt was riding third behind Michael Waltrip and his son Dale Junior, shouting instructions over his radio for both to "Stay low! Stay low!" when his car shot up the track and into the fourth-turn wall. He was killed instantly.

Earnhardt had hired Waltrip, who was winless in 462 starts, during the off-season because he had faith in him. He had promoted his son up to the Winston Cup level a season before for the same reason. That day, both delivered.

Cynics said after the race that Earnhardt was more concerned with blocking the paths of the other drivers than he was in getting the win that day. Utter nonsense. If he was, it would have been the first time in his life.

Bryant McMurray

Harry Gant

"Handsome Harry" Gant, one of
NASCAR's most popular drivers,
went on a four-for-September
winning streak in 1991 that
stands as one of the most
remarkable ever in NASCAR
history. He missed his fifth win
that month when a ten-cent
part broke.

On a Hot Streak

A winning streak in sports is a rare and sometimes beautiful thing to watch. Because of the complexities involved, streaks are more rare in racing than in most other sports. Below are 10 of the more notable streaks.

1. HARRY GANT, 1991

Harry Gant had finished second so many times in his career that they called him "Hard Luck Harry." After 1991, they called him "Mister September."

Beginning with a 10-second victory over Ernie Irvan in the Southern 500 at Darlington on September 1, Gant went on a four-race tear and would not allow anyone else in victory lane.

He slipped by Davey Allison with 19 laps to go in the Miller 400 at Richmond on September 7 to take a four-car-length win, then dominated the Peak Antifreeze 500 at Dover, Delaware, on September 15. In that one, he finished a lap ahead of the field, the first time anyone had done that since May of 1987.

Then Gant capped it off with a come-from-behind win in the Goody's 500 at Martinsville on September 22. He had led 179 of the race's first 356 laps when Rusty Wallace sent him spinning as the two fought for the lead. Even with the damage, Gant retook the lead on lap 454 and held a one-second margin over Brett Bodine at the finish.

A 10-cent part cost Gant a complete sweep of the month. Gant dominated the Holly Farms 400 at North Wilkesboro until his brakes failed due to a malfunctioning O-ring in his brake system. Dale Earnhardt passed him with nine laps to go, but Gant hung on for second place—with no brakes.

2. **RICHARD PETTY, 1967**

There are streaks, and there are unbelievable streaks. Richard Petty's 10-race winning streak in the middle of the 1967 season falls in the latter category.

From August 12, when he led all 250 laps in the Myers Brothers Memorial in Winston-Salem through the Wilkes 400 at North Wilkesboro on October 1, where he finished two laps ahead of the field, Petty was untouchable.

Untouchable? In six of those races, he started on the pole. In two, he was on the outside pole, and he started fifth twice. He finished in a lap by himself eight times, and only one driver, Dick Hutcherson, finished in the same lap during the stretch, at Richmond and Hillsboro, North Carolina.

The fabulous run ended at Charlotte on October 15 when Petty hit Paul Goldsmith on lap 41, ripping his driver's-side door off. He parked it with a blown engine after 268 laps.

3. **JEFF GORDON, 1995–1998**

They call Darlington Raceway the track "too tough to tame," and the Southern 500 the hardest race to win in Winston Cup racing. Tell it to Jeff Gordon.

For four straight Labor Day weekends, the young driver from Pittsboro, Indiana, had Darlington eating out of his hand.

From the time he took a .66-second win over Dale Earnhardt on September 3, 1995, until he ran down and beat Jeff Burton in 1998, no one could touch Gordon at Darlington.

In 1996, Gordon spoiled what would have been one of the greatest upsets in auto-racing history. Journeyman Hut Stricklin, who had not won a Winston Cup race in 217 starts, dominated most of the race, but an overheating problem on his Stavola Brothers Ford gave Gordon the only chance he needed. Gordon passed Stricklin with 16 laps to go and took an easy win.

The next year, Gordon won the Winston Million bonus (for winning three of racing's Big Four races) by holding off Jeff Burton in a fender-banging duel in the final laps of the 1997 Southern 500.

In the 1998 Southern 500, Gordon and fan Jim Chorman of Staten Island each picked up $1 million as part of a "You win, they win" bonus offered by Winston.

4. DARRELL WALTRIP, 1981

Darrell Waltrip spent a fortune buying out his contract with DiGard Racing at the end of the 1980 season, then he turned around and made it all back behind the wheel of Junior Johnson's Chevrolets the next season.

Waltrip was particularly hot in the last half of the campaign, winning seven of the final 14 races, placing second five times, and placing third once. That included a four-race winning string at Martinsville, North Wilkesboro, Charlotte, and Rockingham.

Bryant McMurray

Darrell Waltrip

Darrell Waltrip in victory lane after the 1978 Southeastern 500 at Bristol (Tennessee) International Raceway. Waltrip dominated the high-banked half-mile track, winning seven races in one stretch from 1981-1984. His 12 Bristol victories are the most by one driver at the track.

He coasted to his first Winston Cup championship with 12 wins in 31 races and had enough money left over at the end of the season to buy his new boss a mule named Roadie.

"Every man needs a good mule," Johnson said.

5. **DAVID PEARSON, 1973-1978**

For five and a half years at Charlotte Motor Speedway, if you started a Winston Cup race, you started it behind David Pearson.

Beginning with a pole win for the fall race in 1973, the Spartanburg driver won 11 straight pole positions.

Pearson also won three of those races, including a sweep of the World 600 and National 500 in 1974.

6. **DARRELL WALTRIP, AGAIN**

For a while there at Bristol Motor Speedway, everybody else raced for second place.

Darrell Waltrip, the all-time leading winner at Bristol, "The World's Fastest Half-Mile," put together a string of seven straight wins as part of his 12 wins at the high-banked track.

From the 1981 Valleydale 500 through the same race in 1984, Waltrip did not lose. The streak included four Busch 500 wins, too.

7. **JUNIOR JOHNSON AND FRED LORENZEN, 1961-1965**

This is possibly the wackiest streak in racing history. In 1961, when North Wilkesboro Speedway held its first Grand National Race, hometown boy Junior Johnson won it from the pole. Then he won the next two, also from the pole.

Then the interloper, Illinois native Fred Lorenzen, won the next four—from the pole. Then Johnson won the next

Fred Lorenzen

Bryant McMurray

They called Fred Lorenzen "Fast Freddie," "The Elmhurst Express," and "Golden Boy" during his short but spectacular racing career. The Illinois native showed the Southern boys a thing or two in the 1960s. In 1964, he won 8 of the 16 races he entered and finished 13th in NASCAR Winston Cup points despite not competing in 45 of the 61 races held that year. Lorenzen was the first driver in NASCAR history to earn more than $100,000 in one season ($122,588 in 1963).

two from the pole. Finally, in the 1965 Wilkes 400, Lorenzen won the race—from the pole!

Jim Paschal finally broke up that tea party in 1966 with a win in the Gwyn Staley 400. Do you really have to ask where he started?

8. **FRED LORENZEN, AGAIN**

"Fast Freddy" Lorenzen didn't piddle with the small races, so purists might question the legitimacy of this streak. But the fact remains that Lorenzen won every race he entered between March 22 and May 9, 1964, a total of five wins.

Lorenzen began with a pair of 500-mile wins, in Bristol and Atlanta, skipping the short races at Greenville, South Carolina, and Winston-Salem. He won the Atlanta 500, then skipped four 100-150 mile races. At North Wilkesboro on May 19, he sputtered across the finish line with a blown engine—and a victory.

Then he jumped into USAC territory in a race called the Yankee 300 at the Indianapolis Raceway Park road course and defeated the best they had to offer. Holding his Ford in fourth gear (the only gear he had left) by brute force over the final 10 laps, he beat Parnelli Jones to the checkered flag.

Finally, he breezed by Fireball Roberts to take an easy win in the Rebel 500 at Darlington.

9. **RICK HENDRICK, 1995-1998**

No team owner, not even Junior Johnson, put together a string like Rick Hendrick's four straight championships between 1995 and 1998.

Perhaps even more remarkable is that Hendrick won three of those Winston Cup titles with a talented but untested driver in Jeff Gordon.

Gordon won the 1995 championship in only his third full season, lost to veteran teammate Terry Labonte by 37 points in 1996, then won back-to-back titles in 1997 and 1998.

Don't underestimate the power of inspiration. In November 1996, Hendrick was diagnosed with a rare and virulent form of cancer. If Gordon and Labonte needed inspiration, they didn't have to look any further than the front office.

Hendrick was unable to enjoy much of his team's success as he battled his disease, but in December 1999, it was announced that he was in complete remission. Make that five championships in a row.

10. **CARL KIEKHAFER, 1956**

Team owner Carl Kiekhafer didn't stay in NASCAR long, but they won't forget him for a long, long time.

In two seasons, 1955 and 1956, Kiekhafer's drivers won 52 of 90 races. Of course, he did have the best drivers. And the best equipment. And enough money to burn a wet mule.

Put that up against a bunch of glorified shade-tree mechanics, and it's not hard to figure out how his drivers won 16 straight races between March 23 and June 3, 1956.

Tim Flock, who won 18 races for Kiekhafer in 1955, won one race and then quit due to ulcers. Buck Baker won eight and Speedy Thompson four. The last man to beat a Kiekhafer car, Herb Thomas, was hired by Kiekhafer and added three wins near the end of the string.

Fudgin' with the Rules

For half a century, the knock on NASCAR has been that the association never had a rule it couldn't change. Quite often, NASCAR changed its rules to stay a step ahead of the competitors, some of whom would cheat their grandmothers out of a win. Other times, NASCAR fiddled with the rulebook just to try to make the sport work. For their part, drivers weren't against stretching the rules now and then.

1. BUD MOORE, 1964

Before a race at Martinsville in 1964, team owner Bud Moore was engaged in a spirited discussion on pit road with a NASCAR official who said Moore's car sat too low.

Maurice "Pop" Eargle, one of Moore's crewmen, had the remedy. He found a couple of flat rocks, and while Moore and the official were arguing, dropped them at the front wheels and rolled the car forward a couple of inches.

Then he joined the discussion and told the official that he must have measured wrong. The official measured again, and *voila!* the car was exactly the right height.

He went away scratching his head, and Eargle got rid of the rocks.

Bryant McMurray

Bud Moore

Bud Moore, shown here at Michigan International Speedway in 1979, owned cars that won 63 races in his four-decade career. Moore was also a decorated World War II veteran.

2. **HOSS ELLINGTON, 1976**

Car owner Hoss Ellington, a notorious bender of the rules, fielded two cars for the 1976 National 500 at Charlotte. A. J. Foyt got the primary car but parked it after 59 laps, saying he couldn't keep it in a 10-acre briar patch. Donnie Allison went on to win the race in the second car.

Because of Ellington's reputation, NASCAR chief inspector Bill Gazaway went over Allison's engine with a fine-tooth comb. Someone asked Ellington during the inspection if he was worried. Ellington said, "No problem.... We left all our cheater stuff at Darlington."

3. **JUNIOR JOHNSON, 1965**

Maybe NASCAR figured it owed Junior Johnson one at the 1965 Rebel 300 at Darlington. In 1962, Johnson had been flagged the winner in the Southern 500 but was stripped of his win when it was discovered that Larry Frank had actually completed one more lap.

Johnson's win in the '65 Rebel 300 was protested by car owner Bud Moore, who figured that his driver, Darel Dieringer, should have won it.

Johnson was running away with the race, but on his final pit stop, he slid past his pit box. His crew ran down and serviced the car. Under NASCAR rules, Johnson should have been required to make another lap and stop in the proper space. He didn't.

Two days later, however, NASCAR upheld the win, saying Johnson did not violate the rule because the pit area where he stopped was not being used.

There's an undeniable logic in that. Had the pit been in use at the time, Johnson probably wouldn't have won, anyway.

4. HENLEY GRAY, 1976

If you don't have the money to run with the big boys, you have to use your wits.

When independent driver Henley Gray's car was discovered to have a cleverly hidden bottle of nitrous oxide aboard at Talladega in 1976, Gray happily admitted to using the stuff all the time: "It's the cheapest horsepower you can buy," he said.

5. A NASCAR NO-CALL, 1954

At a 100-miler at Lakewood Speedway in Atlanta on March 21, Herb Thomas nosed out Buck Baker and Dick Rathmann to win the race, or so he thought.

After the race, NASCAR supervisor Johnny Bruner penalized Thomas a lap for not falling in at the rear of the field after a caution-period pit stop.

A few hours later, it was brought to NASCAR's attention that Baker had done the same thing, so he was kicked back. The third-place finisher, Rathmann, was not given the win because he was docked a lap when it was decided that his crew fueled his car while it was partially on the racing surface.

Finally, fifth-place Tim Flock was also penalized a lap because a crewman had wiped some mud off his windshield. That would have made the fourth-place finisher, Gober Sosebee, the winner.

Rather than try to figure the mess out, NASCAR canceled all the penalties and gave Thomas the win.

6. NASCAR AND "THE BANANA," 1966

Faced with the possibility of boycotts by the auto manufacturers in 1966, Bill France, Sr., slackened the rules a bit to keep the big-name drivers and the manufacturers in the game.

When the drivers came to Atlanta on August 7 for the Dixie 400, things had gotten way out of hand. Junior Johnson showed up with a Ford Galaxy that looked nothing like a production model. Painted yellow, the car featured a front end that sloped downward, a "chopped" roofline, and a rear end that was raised considerably to help with aerodynamics.

The car was immediately given the nickname "The Banana," but it miraculously passed inspection.

Smokey Yunick had a tricked-up Chevelle that was a long way off from a street model, but it somehow passed muster, too.

France later admitted that he had sort of set the rulebook aside, but he accomplished his goal of keeping the name drivers and the automakers involved with NASCAR.

7. CURTIS TURNER AND JOE WEATHERLY, 1956

Curtis Turner and his sidekick, Joe Weatherly, were such drawing cards that NASCAR once gave them points for a race they didn't officially start.

On August 12, 1956, both competed in a Grand National race at Elkhart Lake, Wisconsin, and were late arriving at a Convertible division race at Flat Rock, Michigan, that same day.

Officials held up the start as long as they reasonably could, then began the race without them. Fifteen laps later, the pair roared in from the airport, hopped into their cars, and began to race.

Both drivers had mechanical problems and did not finish, but both were credited with starting the race. More important for Turner, he was credited with the 104 points he got for his 13th-place finish.

Points leader Bob Welborn complained that, had it been him, "[NASCAR] would have never given me the points."

8. **THE PETTYS** *ET AL,* **1960**

In NASCAR's defense, the sanctioning body has made some tough calls over the years. In the inaugural World 600 at Charlotte, Lee and Richard Petty and others were disqualified for pitting without using pit road.

These days, there is no penalty for pitting if a driver wipes out in the huge grassy section that separates the track's dog-leg front stretch from the pits, then drives to his pit.

The track was not the only thing that wasn't ready for competition that day. There was no grass where there should have been some, and NASCAR feared a dust storm if any cars cut across the area to pit instead of using pit road.

Junior Johnson was the first to break the rule, plowing through the temporary victory-lane platform that was constructed on the track side of pit road. Johnson figured that as long as he was that close, he'd go ahead and get some gas. Later, Lee Petty did the same thing, missing the victory stand only because Johnson had already taken it out.

Six days later, NASCAR notified the Pettys, Johnson, Paul Lewis, Lennie Page, and Bob Welborn that they had been disqualified. Sorry, boys. No points, no money.

9. **BOBBY ALLISON, 1973**

Bobby Allison figured he'd been cheated out of a win in the National 500 at Charlotte in 1973, and, brother, he let NASCAR know about it.

Allison protested that the engines in winner Cale Yarborough's and second-place Richard Petty's cars were oversized. NASCAR inspected all three of the top finishers, and Allison's engine fit the cubic-displacement specs. Six hours after the inspections began, NASCAR technical director Bill Gazaway told the press that the results were being sent to headquarters in Daytona for a final decision. Allison suspected a cover-up.

Monday afternoon NASCAR released a statement saying that, because the inspection facilities at Charlotte were inadequate, the pre-race inspection numbers would be used—when all three cars were legal—and that the results would stand.

Allison threatened both to quit and to sue. It was not until after a private meeting with NASCAR President Bill France, Jr., a week later that Allison was assuaged.

Speculation was that Allison had been bought off. Allison wouldn't confirm or deny it, saying only that he had "received satisfactory restitution, and you can read that any way you want to."

10. NASCAR AND THE GRAND NATIONAL/TOURING RACE, 1969

Bill France, Sr., faced a tough challenge the week his new monolithic Alabama International Motor Speedway opened for business.

The track surface wasn't smooth enough to race on, and the speeds were so fast that drivers felt their tires wouldn't hold up. It would be unsafe to race. Through their hastily formed Professional Drivers Association, they threatened to boycott the race.

On Saturday afternoon before the September 14 race, after the completion of the 400-mile Grand Touring division race, which featured slower cars, France asked the Grand Touring drivers to stick around. Then, over the garage PA system, he advised everybody who didn't want to race on Sunday to clear out.

Thirty-two cars, including most of the "name" drivers, loaded up and left.

France relaxed the rules, adding 23 Grand Touring cars in behind the 13 Grand National drivers who elected to stick around.

An unknown driver from Rocky Point, North Carolina, named Richard Brickhouse won the race and got full credit for a GN win.

Top 10 Championship Battles

S ome people credit—and blame—NASCAR's current scoring system (in use since 1975) for the tightness of several Winston Cup championship battles. Under the system, consistency is considered as much a virtue as occasional brilliance. Over the years, NASCAR has tried different systems and has seen both good and bad chases. Some of the good ones:

1. ROBERTS VS. REXFORD, 1950

Fireball Roberts came into the final race of NASCAR's second season trailing Bill Rexford by 110.5 points for the championship.

When Rexford succumbed to engine problems early in the 200-mile event at Occoneechee Speedway in Hillsboro, North Carolina, all Roberts needed to do was to soft-pedal it to the finish.

As much as it would add to Roberts's legacy to say that he went for the race win because he was a hard charger, the decision was strictly business. The race paid $1,500 and the championship was worth only $1,000.

It was a gamble he lost on both ends. Roberts's engine failed in the 126th lap, costing him the race. Neither Roberts, who finished 21st, nor 26th-place Rexford earned any points for that race, and Rexford won the championship.

2. **ALLISON VS. ELLIOTT VS. KULWICKI, 1992**

Alan Kulwicki was hardly a blip on the championship radar screen with five races left in the 1992 campaign when he trailed leader Bill Elliott by 191 points. Folks were too busy watching Elliott and Davey Allison duke it out.

But Elliott faltered at Phoenix in the penultimate race, allowing Allison to take the points lead and Kulwicki to move into second place, 30 points behind Allison and 10 points ahead of Elliott.

Allison needed only to finish fifth or better to lock up the title in Atlanta. He got knocked out of the equation. He was running fifth when Ernie Irvan spun and took him into the wall on lap 254.

That accident pared the battle down to two. Elliott was running away with the race, but Kulwicki was hanging on in second place. In the end, it would come down to which driver led the most laps, because the man who leads the most laps in a race is awarded five bonus points.

Elliott won the race, earning 180 points: 175 for first place and a five-point bonus for leading a lap. Kulwicki finished second, also earning 180: 170 points for second place, five for leading a lap, and five for leading the most laps.

Kulwicki led 103 laps, Elliott 102. Had Elliott led one lap more than Kulwicki, the two would have tied for the championship. Since Elliott had five wins and Kulwicki only two, Elliott would have won the championship on the tiebreaker.

But he didn't, and Kulwicki won the title by 10 points, the closest battle in Winston Cup history.

3. **WALLACE VS. EARNHARDT, 1989**

Rusty Wallace had his championship machine on cruise control with two races left in the 1989 season. Then he met Stan Barrett.

Wallace was enjoying a comfortable lead in the final 60 laps at Phoenix when he tried to get around the lapped car driven by Barrett, whose brakes failed at just the wrong moment. They wrecked.

Still, Wallace came into Atlanta needing only to finish within 19 spots of wherever Dale Earnhardt finished to win the title. He would need every one of them.

Wallace started fourth and dropped comfortably back in the pack. When he was among the early leaders to pit, he lost a lap when Greg Sacks crashed. Then Wallace thought he had a flat tire when he didn't, and then lug nuts began to wear through his left rear wheel. He went three laps down.

Earnhardt did all he could. He won the race in dominant fashion, a full 25 seconds ahead of Geoff Bodine. But Wallace hung on for 15th place, giving him the title by 12 points.

"As sloppy as it looked," Wallace said, "this is still the highlight of my career."

4. **WALTRIP VS. ELLIOTT, 1985**

Bill Elliott won everything but the championship. The Georgia native became "Awesome Bill from Dawsonville" in 1985 with 11 victories. He also became the first winner of the "Winston Million" by winning three of stock car racing's four crown-jewel events.

But Darrell Waltrip, the slick-talking driver from Owensboro, Kentucky, spooked Elliott out of the title.

Although Waltrip won only three races, Elliott fell apart down the stretch. He left Darlington in September with a

206-point lead but squandered it with a variety of problems in the final three months of the season. And after every stumble, Waltrip put the screws to his foe.

Elliott faltered at Richmond, Dover, Martinsville, and North Wilkesboro. Waltrip won at Richmond and finished second at Dover and Martinsville. After the Richmond win, which sliced 53 points off Elliott's lead, Waltrip said, "Once I get a guy in sight, I get encouraged."

When Waltrip finished 14th at North Wilkesboro (to Elliott's 30th), he took the points lead and never looked back. He won the title by a healthy 101 points.

5. **MARTIN VS. EARNHARDT, 1990**

Nobody knew it at the time, but the 1990 championship was decided in the second race of the season. By half an inch.

Mark Martin won the Pontiac Excitement 400 at Richmond in the second event of the campaign, but the post-race inspection revealed an infraction in the carburetor of his Ford.

The carburetor was mounted on the engine's intake manifold with an aluminum spacer which was half an inch thicker than the two inches allowed. Had it been welded instead of bolted on, it would have been legal. And had Martin finished fourth or fifth—and not been required to undergo a post-race inspection—the infraction would have never been discovered.

The team was fined $40,000 (the largest in Winston Cup history), but more important, Martin was docked 46 points. That was the difference between first and 10th place, which was the final spot on the lead lap at Richmond.

Martin wound up losing the championship to Dale Earnhardt by 26 points.

6. **GORDON VS. JARRETT, 1997**

Jeff Gordon came into the final race of the 1997 season needing only an 18th-place finish or better to lock up his second championship. He very nearly destroyed his hopes the day before the race.

Going out for the morning practice on Saturday, he goosed his Chevrolet a bit too hard as he came onto pit road. He slid into the pit wall, damaging the car sufficiently to have to go to a back-up car. Then he slipped in qualifying, managing to start only 37th.

Gordon and crew chief Ray Evernham had a powwow. They decided to shoot for a conservative 15th-place finish.

"We had a meeting and said we had two strikes against us and we didn't need to hit a home run," Evernham said. "This is the whole ball game and we just needed a bunt single—or even a foul ball."

Gordon finished 17th and beat Dale Jarrett by 15 points for the crown.

7. **PARSONS VS. YARBOROUGH, 1973**

Nice guys don't always finish last. In fact, in 1973, Benny Parsons went a long way toward disproving that theory.

Thirteen laps into the final race of the season at Rockingham, Parsons could see his 194.35-point advantage over Cale Yarborough lying on the track along with the right side of his car.

Parsons had gotten into a tangle with Johnny Barnes and basically destroyed his race car. Putting it back together became a community project. Scavenging parts off other wrecked cars and getting help from the crewmen of several other teams, Parsons rolled back onto the track 136 laps down. He didn't have much sheet metal on the right side of his car, but he was nonetheless rolling.

He wound up finishing 28th in the 43-car field, thanks to a heavy attrition rate, and beat Yarborough by 67.15 points.

8. **EARNHARDT VS. YARBOROUGH, 1980**

Cale Yarborough closed the gap to within 29 points of Dale Earnhardt by winning the Atlanta Journal 500, and Earnhardt did everything he could to give the 1980 title to Yarborough in the season-ending L.A. Times 500 at Ontario, California.

Earnhardt pitted too soon during a caution period early in the race and lost a lap. He got the lap back, but on a later caution, nearly blew it again. He made his pit stop, intending to get gas only, but his crew began changing his tires. He left his pit with only two lug nuts secured on his right rear wheel and was black-flagged.

He managed to stay in the lead lap, however, and that was enough. He finished fifth to Yarborough's third and took the title by 19 points.

9. **WALTRIP VS. ALLISON, 1981**

Junior Johnson must have given his driver some kind of half-time pep talk. Darrell Waltrip was down by 341 points in June. He cut it to 206 after the Firecracker 400 at Daytona in July, the midpoint of the season.

Then he went on a tear, winning seven of the next 13 races, finishing second five times and third once.

Bobby Allison never knew what hit him. He lost the title by 58 points to Waltrip.

10. **PETTY VS. WALTRIP, 1979**

Bobby Allison taught Darrell Waltrip a lesson in 1979, and it was an expensive one.

The two swapped sheet metal on the 308th lap of the Holly Farms 400 at North Wilkesboro, the 28th race of the 31-race season, and Allison didn't take kindly to the shoving match. He put a fender on Waltrip and sent him head-on into the wall. Nine laps later, Waltrip returned to the track and finished 15th. It would prove to be a critical slip.

Waltrip and Richard Petty traded the points lead twice before the season finale at Ontario, California, and Waltrip entered the race with a two-point lead. Petty finished fifth and Waltrip eighth in the L.A. Times 500, giving Petty his seventh championship by an 11-point margin.

And the lesson for Waltrip?

"He has to learn that when you pass someone, you go around him, not through him," Allison said.

Fanatics

R ace fans are said to be among the most enthusiastic sup-
porters in sports. Sometimes tragically, sometimes com-
ically, that has proven to be true.

1. ASHEVILLE-WEAVERVILLE, 1965

The action was hot and heavy during a 100-mile race at
Asheville-Weaverville Speedway in North Carolina on February 28, 1965. More hot than heavy.

A grass fire sprung up outside the backstretch guardrail
midway through the race, and the caution flag waved to
allow firefighters to extinguish the blaze.

Once the race restarted, however, wind from the speeding cars apparently re-ignited the embers, scorching a strip
20 yards wide and 200 yards long. Some of the 6,500 spectators grabbed shovels, blankets and seat cushions to beat
out the fire as Ned Jarrett sped to victory.

2. GREENVILLE-PICKENS, 1950s–1960s

NASCAR was not always the family sport it is today. Back in
the 1950s and 1960s, the fans were as rough as the drivers
they came to watch.

Sometimes, according to Charleston, South Carolina driver "Little Bud" Moore, they were rougher. And nowhere, Moore noted, were they rougher than at Greenville-Pickens (South Carolina) Speedway.

"They were so mean, you couldn't back up against the pit fence, because the women would cut you with a knife," Moore once said.

That's rough.

3. **MARTINSVILLE, 1957**

A 250-mile race at Martinsville Speedway on May 5, 1957 was red-flagged 59 laps short of the finish due to a freak accident.

Billy Myers was attempting to pass Tom Pistone when their cars collided and Myers's Mercury crashed through the guardrail.

Several fans were standing in an area clearly marked "No Spectators Allowed" when Myers landed right in the middle of them. Five were injured.

4. **POCONO, 1993**

Chad Blaine Kohl was arrested on two felony charges and four misdemeanors after an incident during the running of the Champion Spark Plug 500 at Pocono International Raceway in Pennsylvania on June 13, 1993.

Kohl, 25, leaped over the six-foot fence that separated the racing surface from an infield camping area, ran across the track, and dove over the wall outside the first turn of the 2.5-mile triangular track.

Leaders Kyle Petty and Davey Allison were approaching when Kohl jumped the wall.

"Ever seen a deer frozen in its tracks by headlights?" Petty said. "That pretty much describes what he looked like."

Allison added, "I never believed anybody could be that dumb."

Kohl admitted to the police that he had been drinking beer since 3 a.m.

5. ASHEVILLE-WEAVERVILLE, 1961

Shortly after the Western Carolina 500 at Weaverville, North Carolina, was halted just beyond the halfway point due to a badly disintegrating track, a mob of 10,000 spectators blocked the exit from the pits, trapping the drivers and crews inside. The fans wanted one of two things: More racing or a refund.

Police were unable to disperse the crowd. An impromptu emissary from the infield was sent to negotiate with the crowd; they threw him into a lake.

"Pop" Eargle, a six-foot-six, 342-pound crewman, approached one of the crowd's ringleaders, and was jabbed in the stomach with a 2x4. Big mistake. Eargle grabbed the board and whacked the fan over the head with it. Shortly thereafter, the crowd dispersed.

Four spectators were treated for minor injuries and several were arrested.

6. CHARLOTTE, 1960

Fans loved Junior Johnson, the "Wilkes County Wild Man," for his hard-charging style. All except for one, who might have loved him too much.

In 1960, while practicing for a 100-miler at the Charlotte Fairgrounds, a rough half-mile dirt track, Johnson twice broke rear axles in his Pontiac.

A fan in the infield, who happened to own a 1960 Pontiac like Johnson's, offered to lend Johnson the axle out of his car.

Johnson took him up on it and things went well for a few laps. He started 20th and was roaring his way up through the pack. On the 37th lap, as he was attempting to pass Rex White for the lead, his axle snapped.

History does not record if Johnson replaced the fan's axle.

7. NORTH WILKESBORO, 1957

Tiny Lund, driving a Pontiac owned by J.S. Rice, was involved in a freak accident that took the life of a spectator during a 100-mile Grand National race at North Wilkesboro Speedway on October 20, 1957.

In the second half of the race, the rear axle on Lund's car broke and a loose wheel off his car bounded over the fence into the grandstands, killing W.R. Thomason of Mt. Holly, North Carolina.

8. WILMINGTON, DELAWARE, SOMEWHERE IN TIME

Before he came south to head up the mechanical side of the famous Holman-Moody teams of the 1960s, Ralph Moody was something of a vagabond, racing all over his native New England.

Moody had come up with an innovation, only slightly illegal, that hopped up his little Sportsman car so much that it would outrun even the big modifieds. When he did just that at Wilmington, Delaware, once—he doesn't remember the date—the promoter was so convinced Moody was cheating that he refused to pay Moody and banned him from the track.

Moody plotted his revenge. He went to a local scrap-iron lot, bought an old junker, and installed his equipment under the hood. He had a friend take it to the track and enter a race. When Moody showed up as a spectator, the friend asked the promoter if Moody could drive his car.

Not seeing the heap as much of a threat, the promoter said okay. Moody blew the field away. The promoter disqualified him.

When the fans heard about the disqualification, Moody said, they became so incensed that they burned the grandstands down. He swore it was true.

9. LAKEWOOD, 1949

NASCAR's first season was officially over and Red Byron crowned the champion when promoter Sam Nunis announced that he was hosting a 150-mile Strictly Stock race at the brand-new Lakewood Speedway in Atlanta.

NASCAR president Bill France quickly offered his help, saying that all the NASCAR drivers would be eligible for the race, though it would not carry any points.

Tim Flock won the race, but the event was marred when his brother Bob lost a wheel off his Oldsmobile. The wheel caromed into the crowd and broke both legs of 11-year-old fan Buster Henley.

10. RIVERSIDE, CALIFORNIA, 1965

Dick Powell's spin off the track during the 1965 running of the Motor Trend 500 on the road course at Riverside had a freak, tragic consequence.

Several fans sitting on a forklift parked near the first and second turns of the 2.7-mile course leaned too quickly to see the spin. The sudden shift in weight caused the forklift to overturn and roll down a hill.

Three spectators were injured and 20-year-old Ronald Pickle of San Diego was killed.

Building a Better Mousetrap

N ASCAR teams have never had trouble making their cars fast, but finding ways to make cars safe at high speeds has proven difficult. Most innovations in racing have tried to address this challenge.

1. "POP" EARGLE'S CHECK-VALVE

When Johnny Allen's Pontiac turned upside down in the 1962 Southern 500, the spilled gas caught fire. Someone said something ought to be done.

Maurice "Pop" Eargle, a six-foot-six, 342-pound mechanic who worked out of Cotton Owens's garage, sent NASCAR a solution two days later.

Eargle took a one-inch steel ball from a pinball machine, put it in a wire strap within the fuel fill pipe, and made, in effect, a check-valve. When the car was upright, the ball allowed fuel to be poured in. When the car was upside-down, the ball closed the pipe to prevent gas from spilling. Eargle's simple innovation did much to lessen the threat of fire, the drivers' greatest fear.

By 1963, Eargle's check-valve was standard equipment on all the cars.

2. **RADIOS**

Today, virtually every member of a Winston Cup team is equipped with a headset. The driver, crew chief, and spotter are in constant communication via radio. Each crewman wears a headset to help coordinate pit stops.

The first recorded use of two-way radios was on February 9, 1952, in a modified-Sportsman race on Daytona's beach-road course. Driver Al Stevens of Odenton, Maryland, who operated a radio-dispatched wrecker service, stationed two friends in cars with radios at each end of the course. He had one in his car and a fourth in his pit. Stevens noted after the race that they were a tremendous help in avoiding spin-outs and pileups.

3. **FUEL CELL**

Legend has it that either Ralph Moody or Smokey Yunick, two of the most ingenious mechanics in racing, designed the first fuel cell but could not get NASCAR to approve it. Wherever the fuel cell came from, it was a lifesaver.

The fuel cell, basically, is a rubber bladder inside the metal fuel tank of a race car. It is designed to stay intact in crashes in which the fuel tank ruptures.

The first fuel cell approved by NASCAR, in 1965, was developed by Firestone.

4. **TIRE SAFETY InnER LInER**

With the advent of the superspeedway era (beginning with the construction of Daytona International Speedway in 1959), speeds increased dramatically simply because the tracks were bigger.

Racers needed something to lessen the danger of blowouts, so Goodyear came up with a "tire-within-a-tire" concept in 1965. Instead of an inner tube, which blew when a tire blew, a second, smaller tire was mounted inside the tire that touched the pavement.

The key to the concept's success was that each tire was inflated independently (i.e., with its own valve stem) so that if the outer tire blew, the inner tire would remain inflated. The inner tire was not designed to last for more than a couple of laps, but it did give a driver the ability to steer his car after a blowout.

5. "SEVERE USAGE KITS"

For the first couple of NASCAR seasons, Bill France, Sr., was adamant that the cars be "stock"—race cars were not allowed to have any parts on them that were not available to the driving public.

By 1953, it was evident that the heavy race cars were overtaxing some parts, so the Hudson, Lincoln, and Oldsmobile manufacturers began supplying "severe usage kits" with beefed-up hubs, axles, wheel spindles, and suspension systems. The parts were built for race cars, but anyone could buy them.

6. RACING TIRES

Until 1952, race-car drivers got their tires where everyone else did: down at the service station.

In 1952, Pure Oil Company, one of the first companies to become affiliated with NASCAR, developed a racing tire designed specifically for stock cars.

The tire featured an all-nylon cord and sold for $37.90.

7. **"RACING SLICKS"**

After the driver boycott of the 1969 Talladega 500, which was largely attributable to unsafe tires, Junior Johnson went to the huge track six weeks later with his driver, LeeRoy Yarbrough, to test tires for Goodyear.

At that time, only tires with treads were allowed. The Goodyear technicians had brought a set of no-tread, slick tires, and Johnson told them to strap the slicks onto his car. The Goodyear reps said it was useless because they were against the rules.

Johnson told them that if the slicks worked, Bill France, Sr., would approve them. The tires held up much better than the treaded tires.

Based on the results of the test, NASCAR approved the slick tires and they have been in use ever since.

8. **CARBURETOR RESTRICTOR PLATES**

There are as many ways to slow a race car down as there are to speed one up. One of the most successful methods used by NASCAR is the carburetor restrictor plate. It is successful because a) it costs practically nothing to make, b) it is relatively easy to police, and c) it works.

The plate is just that, a roughly 5x5-inch aluminum plate with four holes drilled in it, placed between the carburetor and the engine. The idea is to limit the amount of air taken into the engine's combustion chambers, limiting the amount of fuel that can be burned and therefore limiting horsepower.

The misconception that most fans have is that the plate is a relatively new idea. In 1970, when qualifying speeds for the spring race at Talladega reached nearly 200 mph,

NASCAR required a restrictor plate at all tracks (beginning with the August race at Brooklyn, Michigan) for the remainder of the season.

From 1971–1987, other methods were used to keep speeds down, but when Bobby Allison's car nearly flew into the grandstands at Talladega on May 3, 1987, NASCAR brought the plates back. They have been in use at Talladega and Daytona, the two fastest tracks, ever since.

In the 2000 season, after the deaths of two drivers at New Hampshire International Speedway, NASCAR mandated the plates for that track, also.

9. ROOF FLAPS

Until 1994, everything that went into the design of a race car was built with the intent of creating as much downforce as possible to keep the car planted on the track. The problem with that strategy was that once a car got sideways—or worse, backward—everything that created downforce now created lift. At a high enough rate of speed, the rear end of the car would be lifted off the ground, sometimes with disastrous results.

Some of the brightest minds in racing went to work on the problem. What they came up with were two flaps, roughly eight inches high and 20 inches wide, which were installed over the rear windows on the car's roof. The flaps were hinged on the forward side so that they would lie flat under normal conditions but would open to about a 45-degree angle when a car started spinning.

The flaps counteracted the lift, and the cars, for the most part, have stayed on the ground.

10. **"PERMAPROOF FYRE SAFE FISHER FABRIC" RACING SUIT**

Jimmy Florian won a race shirtless. Fonty Flock won wearing Bermuda shorts. In the early days, drivers often dressed in T-shirts and jeans.

In 1952, Treesdale Laboratories of Pittsburgh introduced the first "fireproof" race wear. The company's baggy "Permaproof Fyre Safe Fisher Fabric" coveralls became an immediate hit. At $9.25 a pair, they were expensive, but did offer a degree of protection from fire.

Weird at the Wire

In theory, a good race ends with two cars battling neck-and-neck down to the checkered flag. In reality, they don't always go like that.

1. CURTIS TURNER

Curtis Turner was noted for winning races by beating and banging his way to the front. On September 30, 1956, in a NASCAR Convertible race at Asheville-Weaverville Speedway, Turner won instead by merely rising above the fray.

On the 181st lap of the 200-lap race, Turner had just slipped into the lead when bedlam broke loose behind him. Of the 14 cars still running in the 24-car field, Turner was the only one to miss the big wreck.

He was named the winner when he wove his way through the tangle of cars and came back to his pit. The race was stopped.

It was the only time in NASCAR history that a race ended with only one car running.

2. MARSHALL TEAGUE

On February 10, 1952, the annual race on the beach-road course at Daytona was cut from 200 miles to 151.7 because the tide was coming in.

The tides often dictated the starting time of races at Daytona, but that day NASCAR officials underestimated the length of time needed to get the 20,000 spectators parked along the beach.

The race was scheduled for 48 laps. The decision to cut it to 37 came with 10 to go.

Marshall Teague, who'd been planning a late pit stop, backed off his accelerator and won the race without having to refuel his big Hudson. The car went dry at the checkered flag.

3. LEE PETTY

You might call it the race that never was, but Lee Petty would have called it something else.

On August 4, 1956, in a little half-mile dustbowl in Tulsa, 32 laps of a scheduled 100-miler were in the books when the track became so clouded with dust that Petty stopped his car in the pits, sprinted across the track, jumped up on the flagstand, and red-flagged the race himself.

Officials apparently agreed with Petty's decision. The race was halted, spectators received a refund, and the race was not rescheduled.

4. BOBBY ALLISON

Sometimes racing is just too easy.

In the fall of 1967, Fred Lorenzen, recently retired from driving, kept badgering the Ford people to bankroll a car for him. Ford finally relented, and Lorenzen went out and got a car that Mario Andretti had used as a spare. Then Lorenzen hired Bobby Allison, who had just been fired by the Chrysler factory team.

In their debut race, the American 500 at Rockingham in October, it proved to be a good match. Allison outlasted the hot-shoes and cruised into a comfortable one-lap lead.

Lorenzen flashed a message on the pit board: Slow Down. Allison did, but not enough to suit Lorenzen, who was afraid the engine would blow. Second message: Slow down some more.

When Allison took the checkered flag, he had both hands clasped behind his head—off the steering wheel!

5. FONTY FLOCK

Truman Fontello "Fonty" Flock, the middle brother in racing's flying circus, had more fun than perhaps any driver who ever lived. When he won, he celebrated.

His sense of fun was never more evident than when he won the 1952 Southern 500 at Darlington. Flock took the checkered flag, dismounted at the start-finish line, and climbed up onto the roof of the car.

The Ft. Payne, Alabama, native then led the crowd of 32,000 in the singing of "Dixie."

Did we mention that he was also wearing Bermuda shorts?

6. DICK RATHMANN

Never let it be said that Dick Rathmann was not a man to be reckoned with on a racetrack.

In 1952, one week after Rathmann came from 22nd place to win a 250-lap race in Oakland, making him NASCAR's first last-to-first winner, he won a race on the other side of the country—on three wheels.

On April 4 at North Wilkesboro, Rathmann blew a tire with two laps to go. This was long before the invention of the tire safety inner liner, and Rathmann's wheel went down on the rim.

He disdained a pit stop and wrestled his big Hudson around the track, kicking up a fine spray of dirt, for the final two circuits. He beat a hard-charging Herb Thomas by 20 seconds at the checkered flag.

7. **LEE PETTY**

It was more a testament to the track conditions than his bravery during the race, but Lee Petty actually won a 200-lap race at a faster pace than that at which he had qualified.

On June 19, 1955, Petty won at Airborne Speedway in Plattsburg, New York, at an average speed of 59.074 mph. He had earlier won the pole position on the soggy half-mile dirt track with a lap of 55.744 mph.

That was the first (and last) time that has ever happened.

8. **BROTHER AGAINST BROTHER AGAINST...**

Brother combinations have been around in NASCAR since its first race in 1949, but in 1952, a fraternal finish defied the odds.

Fonty Flock and Herb Thomas, both members of NASCAR's early family acts, finished first and second in a 100-mile race at Raleigh Speedway on September 30.

What made the race unusual was that Fonty's brother Tim finished third, and Herb's brother Donald finished fourth.

In over a half-century of racing, that particular pecking order among siblings has never been matched.

9. **DAVID PEARSON**

The 1961 Dixie 400 at Atlanta might well be called the race no one wanted to win. The race had four different leaders in the last five laps. In itself, this circumstance was not unusual; it was how the lead changed hands that was the corker.

When Nelson Stacy's engine blew with 24 laps left, the lead went to Banjo Matthews, and he appeared to be headed for an easy win. But with five laps left, smoke erupted from his car, and he was out.

Fireball Roberts then inherited the lead. Even with a clutch that was slipping badly, it appeared as if "Balls" would pull it off. Then, with two laps left, he ran out of gas.

That gave the lead to Bunkie Blackburn, who was driving in relief of Junior Johnson, on the white-flag lap. Then Blackburn slowed in the backstretch, also out of fuel.

David Pearson, who was being scored a lap down, passed Blackburn, but the checkered flag waved for Blackburn. Pearson immediately protested. An hour-long check of the scoring cards proved Pearson right. He had taken the lead. It was the only lap he led all day, but it was the one that counted.

10. **HERB THOMAS**

NASCAR is much too sophisticated for such a thing these days, but at a race in Macon, Georgia, in 1952, the drivers actually voted on whether they wanted to race.

Heavy rains fell on Central City Speedway, but the promoters were determined to give the fans a show. They dried the track as best they could, but the drivers weren't all convinced it was ready. They put it to a vote. By a straw poll of 15–13, they raced.

Darkness shortened the race from 300 laps to 198, and Herb Thomas was the winner. It can only be assumed that he was one of the "ayes."

not Your Father's Oldsmobile

S ince 1949, nearly every brand of American-made car—and, some foreign makes as well—has raced in NASCAR. Some makes served with distinction; some stood out for other reasons.

1. TUCKER TORPEDO

The fifth race of the 1950 Grand National season, paired opposite the Indianapolis 500 on Memorial Day, was quite appropriately called the "Poor Man's 500."

Run in Canfield, Ohio, the race also featured the first and probably only appearance by the Tucker Torpedo. Even though the car, which was driven by Joe Merola, was two years old, it was likely more advanced than any other in the field.

It just wasn't much of a race car. The Tucker Torpedo died before Merola completed a lap.

2. VOLKSWAGEN

The International Stock Car Grand Prix at Langhorne Speedway in 1956 was one of only two races in NASCAR history in which foreign-made vehicles were allowed.

Among the 38-car field were six Jaguars, a pair of Porsches, an Aston-Martin and—believe it or not—a Volkswagen.

Local driver Dick Hagey qualified his Bug at 48 mph, some 16 mph slower than pole winner Lloyd Shaw's Jag, but Hagey puttered around to bag 19th place.

Shaw's Jaguar, incidentally, never led a lap and finished four spots behind Hagey's VW.

3. JAGUAR

The International 100, the first road race in Grand National history, was run on a two-mile course set up around the Linden, New Jersey, airport on June 13, 1954.

It was also the only GN race ever won by a foreign-made car. Al Keller drove his Jaguar hardtop around Herb Thomas's Hudson on the 23rd lap of the 50-lap race and won going away.

In the field that day, which was open to international competition, were 13 Jags, five MGs, an Austin-Healy, a Porsche, and a Morgan.

4. CHEVROLET

In 1955, Chevrolet jumped into auto racing in a big way, advertising-wise. And though Chevies won only two races that season, Herb Thomas was driving one when he won the Southern 500, the biggest stock car race in the country.

The Red Bowtie bunch pounced upon the opportunity, whisking the car away to the Texas State Fair in Dallas, making it the first "show car" in history.

5. WEATHERLY'S "PURPLE PIG"

Joe Weatherly was mired in a deep slump late in the 1955 campaign when he tried to change his luck by changing his paint scheme. He painted his brand-new 1956 Schwam Motors Ford a deep purple and nicknamed it the "Purple Pig."

He finished fourth in a 100-miler at North Wilkesboro in the Purple Pig's first outing, on October 23. It turned out to be Weatherly's best race of the season.

6. THE "e-BIRD"

Bill Elliott's crew wasn't *too* nervous when it was preparing to run for the Winston Million at Darlington on Labor Day weekend of 1985.

Somehow, they turned around the big roof decal on Elliott's Coors Thunderbird during its application. Instead of "9," Elliott's number, the folks in the infield scoring stand saw a lowercase "e" every time Elliott rolled by. To the folks in the grandstands, it looked like a backward "6." There was no way you could turn the car to make it read "9."

The car is still on display at the Joe Weatherly Stock Car Museum at Darlington.

Elliott won, by the way.

7. NASH AMBASSADOR

Nashes were noted more for their sturdiness than for their fleetness afoot, but one actually won a Grand National race.

Curtis Turner drove a factory-backed Nash Ambassador to victory in a 150-lap race at Charlotte Speedway in 1951.

The date, appropriately enough, was April 1.

8. MR. X.

Frank Mundy, one of the few drivers who flew to his races in the 1950s, arrived at the Carrell Speedway near Los Angeles to learn that his race-car hauler had broken down en route.

Mundy went to a local rental shop and rented a car. He watercolored an "X" on the side and finished eighth without a pit crew, extra tires, or gas. Mundy won $100 and the rental car cost only $37, so he cleared $63 on the venture.

9. HENRY J.

Fans came early to the races at Columbia Speedway in the 1950s—not to get a good seat, but to watch the water truck. The burly guy responsible for wetting down the half-mile dirt track drove as if the hounds of hell were on his heels.

One night, an amateur driver in one of the lower divisions showed up at the track with a Henry J, intent on making a preliminary race. He didn't. During the warm-ups, he was passed twice by the water wagon. The amateur driver was out of there long before the green flag ever flew.

There were other Henry J's in other races, but not at Columbia.

10. AIR-CONDITIONED HARDTOP

In the first NASCAR Convertible division race, run on the sands of Daytona Beach in 1956, one hardtop Ford was allowed in the field.

Driven by Pete Peterson, an auto air-conditioning salesman from Chicago, the car started dead last in a field of 28 but wound up 10th.

Peterson, elated, predicted that all the cars would have air conditioning by the Southern 500 on Labor Day.

His prediction didn't work out. To date, Peterson may have driven the only air-conditioned car to ever run a NASCAR race.

They Just Didn't Give a Damn

Racing professionals were not always the public-relations-minded creatures that fans see today, smiling for the cameras. In the early days of NASCAR, they actually had personalities. They pretty well did as they pleased, too.

1. CONVERTIBLE OR HARDTOP, TINY?

DeWayne "Tiny" Lund and Curtis Turner were at opposite ends of the spectrum in racing. Lund was a hardscrabble independent who relied on racing to make a living, and Turner was a wealthy guy who didn't mind tearing up equipment—his or yours—to win.

Once, at a race at Lakewood Speedway in Atlanta, Turner destroyed Lund's car, and Lund hung around until after the race. Then he went after Turner.

Tiny, who stood six-foot-five and weighed about 280 pounds, picked Turner up, carried him to the big lake that covered Lakewood's infield, and proceeded to drown him.

Well, maybe Tiny wouldn't have actually drowned ol' Pops, but no one knew for sure—least of all, Pops.

After about the fifth dunking, Turner got himself off the hook by promising to replace Lund's car.

2. AND YOUR POINT WOULD BE?

As a race-car driver, Junior Johnson knew only one speed: flat out. While the fans loved it, some of the men he drove for didn't.

When Fred Lorenzen gave up the lead with engine problems in the 1961 Virginia 500 Sweepstakes race at Martinsville, Johnson had it made.

No one could catch him, but still he kept the hammer down. Pit-board messages didn't help. When Johnson came in for his final pit stop, car owner Rex Lovette threatened Johnson with a sledgehammer, ordering him to take it easy.

The order went against Johnson's grain, but a sledgehammer is a sledgehammer. Johnson backed off and still won the race by four laps.

3. THINKING OF YOU

Famed mechanic Smokey Yunick stayed in hot water because he called a spade a spade. He'd as soon beard the giant—NASCAR—as not. If Smokey didn't like something, he didn't mind telling everybody.

One of his least favorite people was car owner Carl Kiekhafer. Kiekhafer owned Mercury Outboard Motors. He was a millionaire who spent a lot of money to see his teams win at a time when most teams scrimped by from race to race.

For years, Yunick kept a photo of Kiekhafer over the commode at his shop's bathroom.

4. AND THE WINNER IS . . .

Most racers weren't above a little side bet now and then. According to Smokey Yunick, his two drivers each had one going at Darlington in 1957.

Bryant McMurray

Smokey Yunick

Smokey Yunick ran "The Best Damn Garage in Town" in Daytona Beach, Florida—it said so on the sign right out front. He also built some of the best race cars on the NASCAR circuit. Not always legal, mind you, but fast.

Paul Goldsmith, driving one of Yunick's Chevrolets, had gotten up with a crowd of gamblers and bet them he wouldn't lead the first lap. He'd had the fastest qualifying speed. The problem was, Yunick's other driver was Curtis Turner, who had a similar wager going with another set of bettors. Turner had qualified third, right behind Goldsmith.

When the two came off the fourth turn on the first lap, Goldsmith was standing on his brakes, trying to get Turner to pass. Turner was standing on the gas, trying to push Goldsmith past the flagstand.

It worked out well. Cotton Owens slipped around both and led the first lap.

5. ONE-AND-A-HALF GAINER, WITH A TWIST

It's called making the best of a bad situation.

Before Cale Yarborough hit the big time, he was racing in a Limited Sportsman race on the tiny little bullring called Ashwood Speedway, in Bishopville, South Carolina.

He crashed, and his car went into a lake. Yarborough crawled out of the window, climbed up on the car's roof, and executed a lovely swan dive into the pond.

"I got wet when I flipped, so I figured I might as well have a swim," he reasoned.

6. A ROCK-SLINGIN' GOOD TIME

The first thing you have to understand was that Tiny Lund wouldn't let anybody pass him without earning it, no matter how slow he was going.

In the 1964 Concord 250 in North Carolina, Lund's car wasn't up to snuff, and "Little Joe" Weatherly kept trying to pass. After several tries, Weatherly got impatient and gave

Lund a nudge. The next time Weatherly tried, Tiny carried him into the wall, nearly wrecking them both.

Bud Moore, the owner of Weatherly's car—and a man given to the occasional fit of temper himself—found a good-sized rock in the pits. The next time Lund came by, Moore bounced the rock off Lund's car.

After the race, knowing Lund outweighed his driver by about 100 pounds, Moore slipped a wrench into his pocket before he sauntered over. Fortunately, fans got between the two contestants and the confrontation ended without more serious damage.

7. NOT EXACTLY A BONUS

Crew chief Herb Nab didn't exactly gain favor with the team boss in the 1964 Rebel 300 at Darlington, even after his driver, Fred Lorenzen, won the race. *Especially* after he won the race.

Lorenzen was driving one of the two Holman-Moody Fords in the race, and John Holman believed that the Ford executives he was entertaining would rather see Fireball Roberts in victory lane than Lorenzen.

In the late stages, when the two were running neck-and-neck, Holman sent word to Nab to have Lorenzen pit for gas, which would have effectively blown his chances of winning. Nab responded that he didn't come to Darlington to finish second, and he kept Lorenzen on the track.

When Lorenzen took the checkered flag, it was quickly followed by a pink slip for Nab.

Fortunately for Holman-Moody, cooler heads prevailed and Nab was rehired two days later.

8. BACKInG InTO A WIn(nER)

Bobby Allison was an up-and-comer when he ran afoul of established star Curtis Turner at Bowman Gray-Stadium in Winston-Salem one night.

Turner was leading and Allison couldn't get by, despite several tries. Turner eventually got fed up, let Allison pass, then spun him out, wrecking Allison's car.

Turner went on to win the race and stopped his car at the start-finish line. A few minutes later, fans standing behind Turner's car scattered. Allison had turned his car around at the end of the third turn and slammed it into reverse. He sailed full-tilt into the back end of Turner's car.

q. EXCUSE ME, MA'AM

In the old days, drivers sometimes bunked in together in order to save money. Cale Yarborough and Tiny Lund were an incongruous-looking pair, but frequent roommates.

One weekend when they were sharing a room, they were horsing around the motel pool. Tiny had a distinct height advantage, so he delighted in dunking the feisty Yarborough.

When Lund went inside to take a shower, Yarborough got his revenge. He took the trash can out of the room, filled it half-and-half with ice and water, then stirred it long enough to get the maximum effect. He sneaked back into the room and dumped the whole thing on Lund.

Stark naked, Lund tore out after Yarborough, chasing him through the motel parking lot until he ran smack into the proverbial "little old lady," who, from all reports, came up to about Lund's navel. It was only then that Lund came to his senses.

10. **HIGH AND DRY IN PHOENIX**

Driver George Seeger and his car owner, Tony Sampro, were driving home to California after Seeger's respectable 25th-place finish (out of a field of 82) in the 1951 Southern 500 when they got into an argument.

They stopped at a gas station in Phoenix, and when Seeger went to the rest room, Sampro left him flat.

Country When Country Wasn't Cool

I t was NASCAR before there was a NASCAR.

As the South dug its way out of the Great Depression, a strain of brave, even foolhardy, men paved the way for the Winston Cup stars of today.

Their story was written all over the United States, but nowhere more fetchingly than on the sands at Daytona Beach. From the time a gentleman named Ransom E. Olds blistered the packed sands at 50 mph in 1902 until Robert "Red" Byron took the checkered flag for the final race prior to the incorporation of the National Association for Stock Car Auto Racing in 1948, racers played on the beach at Daytona.

Below are some of the forgotten heroes and events of that era.

1. THE FIRST "STOCK CAR" RACE On THE BEACH

When Sir Malcolm Campbell and his buddies moved their world land-speed record attempts from Daytona to the Bonneville Salt Flats in the mid-1930s, the city fathers of

Daytona wanted to maintain the little resort town's reputation as the "World Center of Speed."

In 1936, they decided that a race would be run on a four-mile course to be built connecting the beach and Highway A1A. The field would consist of American-made stock cars in four classes according to their price tags, ranging from $665-under to $1,301-over.

There were 19 Fords, an Oldsmobile, a Lincoln Zephyr, two Willys 77s, a pair of huge Auburn roadsters, and a Chevrolet. They were piloted by everyone from 1934 Indianapolis 500 winner "Wild Bill" Cummings to Major Goldie Gardner, the mayor of Daytona.

The start was staggered according to qualifying speeds, and some of the slower cars completed several laps before the faster ones ever took the green flag.

The rules, particularly the one involving assistance to disabled cars, went out the window. Every car in the field was mired in the soft turns at least once.

The race was run on March 8, 1936, and it was a wild one. Mayor Gardner parked his Zephyr after a few laps, saying the track was like an obstacle course with all the disabled cars strewn about.

Four hours, 54 minutes, and 42 seconds after the green flag, the race was halted because of the incoming tide. Milt Marion was declared the winner, despite having been bogged down five times.

It was a fiasco. The city lost $22,000 and wanted no more of racing on the beach.

2. BILL FRANCE, 1938

William H. G. "Big Bill" France was among the drivers in the field in that first race in 1936. France, a 25-year-old service-station owner who had moved to Daytona Beach from Washington, D.C., in 1934, drove in races all over the South.

Not only was he a good racer, but he had a knack for promotion. When support for a race in 1937 flagged, France and Charlie Reese, a local nightclub owner, picked up the gauntlet, staging two races in 1938.

The first was run on July 10 and won by Danny Murphy of Ormond Beach. When he claimed the 150.4-mile race at 66.581 mph, he pocketed $300 for first place and $55 in lap prizes. After paying the purse, the lap money, and the city for its assistance, France and Reese split the $200 profit.

On Labor Day, a shady local character named Smokey Purser won the race, then disappeared with the winning car before the post-race inspection. The drivers voted to disqualify Purser. That left France, who finished second, the winner. Reese and France gave first-place money to Lloyd Moody, who had finished third, and France took the second-place check, thus avoiding any hint of impropriety. Racing on the beach was there to stay, for a while, at least.

3. THE ELKS

When the City of Daytona Beach bailed out after the flop of 1936, France asked the Elks Club to sponsor a tripleheader that featured motorcycles, *race cars,* and stock cars, in 1937. Flop number two. Despite spending less than $100 on the promotion, the Elks said they lost money and would not be interested in sponsoring another race in 1938.

4. SMOKEY PURSER, THE "SEA LAWYER"

Smokey Purser was a mysterious figure around Daytona Beach. He owned the New Yorker Bar & Grill, which was a hangout for racers who passed through Daytona Beach.

Most folks figured it was a convenient front for Purser's other, more shady ventures.

When Purser's kids were asked to fill out a questionnaire at school that required listing their parents' occupations, he gave them instructions to say he was a "merchant." Pressed on the subject by one of his daughters, he told her he was a "sea lawyer." Later in life, the daughter figured that it meant her dad handled "cases" at sea.

On the beach-road course, however, Purser was the best.

He won the 1937 race in a field of mostly local racers and from that day until World War II halted the races, he finished in the top five in eight of the 11 races in which he competed. He won two and finished second twice.

5. FIRST—AND ONLY—POWDERPUFF RACE

"An even dozen girls will risk their pretty little necks for gold and glory," read a report in the local newspaper before the Labor Day beach-road race in 1940.

To spice up the show, Bill France had decided to host a "Powderpuff Race" the day before the main event. The entrants, 13 in all, included his wife Anne; Betty Vogt, the wife of "Red" Vogt, the local mechanic who'd later be credited with giving NASCAR its name; and Ethel Flock Mobley, sister of the racing Flock brothers.

France said that, for safety's sake, the top speed allowed on the highway side of the racetrack would be 40 mph. That rule, along with most of the others, was roundly ignored.

Evelyn Reed, of Daytona, took the win in the eight-lap race at an average speed of 68.4 mph. She claimed the munificent sum of $50 for her victory.

6. **WAS SHE FROM PASADEΠA?**

There were two pickup trucks entered in the 1940 Labor Day race. The one driven by George Ruse, Jr., was headed for a top-10 finish until the final lap. As he was barreling toward the checkered flag, an elderly lady—for reasons unknown—walked across the track, stumbled, and fell directly in his path.

Ruse swerved to avoid her, got stuck in the sand, and finished out of the money.

7. **"RAPID ROY" AND "LIGHTΠIΠ' LLOYD"**

Two of the more interesting characters to race on the beach were a couple of cousins from Georgia named Roy Hall and Lloyd Seay.

Hall's appearances in the pre-war races were sporadic, as he often spent time "with the government." Back in his hometown of Atlanta, he was known as an absolutely fearless hauler of moonshine from the North Georgia hills, and his heroic style of driving carried over to the racecourse. In his first Daytona race on March 10, 1940, Hall—quite frequently taking the turns on two wheels—won easily. He also won again, after a brief stay in the Georgia state penitentiary, in 1941.

Seay drove with the same reckless abandon as his cousin, whether it was on the racetrack or hauling 'shine through the hills around Dawsonville and Dahlonega, Georgia.

In his first attempt on the beach-road course, Seay flipped three times, once during practice and twice in the race on March 2. He came back to win the final race of the pre-war years, on August 24, 1941, but it would be his only victory on the beach.

On September 1, only hours after winning a race at Lakewood Speedway, the big dirt track in Atlanta, Seay was shot to death by a cousin, Woodrow Anderson. The two had gotten into an argument over who was to pay a bill for sugar used in the family's illegal whiskey business.

8. "HE DOTH PROTEST TOO MUCH"

Joe Littlejohn, a driver/promoter from Spartanburg, finished third in the Labor Day race in 1940 and immediately protested that the cars driven by winner Buck Mathis and second-place Smokey Purser were not legal.

Bill France had planned to tear down the engines of the top three finishers anyway. The post-race inspection revealed that none of the three were strictly stock. Faced with the unsavory proposition of having to disqualify all three, France declared all three legal.

Littlejohn sheepishly offered to let France keep his third-place winnings if France would return his $25 protest fee and $3 entry fee.

9. ROBERT "RED" BYROn

Red Byron came back from the Second World War with a shattered leg from having been shot down while on a bomb-ing mission, but he was still filled with a passion for speed. He would slake his thirst on the beach, winning three of the six races staged between 1946 and the formation of NASCAR in 1948.

His first victory, on April 14, 1946, was a hot duel with Roy Hall. Hall was leading until he headed for the north turn in the 16th lap. The spectators, many of whom stood on the strand, kept inching inland to avoid the incoming tide. Screaming along the beach, Hall had a decision to make: Turn left and risk sliding into the crowd, or turn right and get wet. He dove into the surf.

Hall recovered and even passed Byron again for the lead but threw a wheel in the south turn, ending his day. Byron cruised to an easy win over Joe Littlejohn.

Byron also won the final pre-NASCAR beach-road race, on February 15, 1948, six days before the organization was incorporated.

10. "LAP PRIZES" AND "BUNDLES FOR BRITAIN"

As a means of getting the citizens involved, Bill France asked local firms to donate money or goods as prizes for drivers leading specific laps. For instance, the leader of the 25th lap in the Labor Day show in 1940 received a case of Pabst Blue Ribbon beer. The leader of the 28th lap got a box of Hav-A-Tampa cigars, courtesy of the Eli Witt Cigar Company. Most were $5 cash prizes.

In 1941, as the war in Europe heated up, the Daytona Beach Exchange Club established a relief fund for the "Bundles for Britain" campaign. Smokey Purser, filled with patriotic fervor, announced that he would donate half his winnings to that campaign and to Greek relief organizations, and he asked the other racers to step up to the plate.

Bill France and Charlie Reese, who were co-promoting the race along with Purser, agreed to donate 25 percent of the net proceeds to Bundles for Britain.

Bibliography

Bledsoe, Jerry. *The World's Number One, Flat-Out, All-Time Great, Stock Car Racing Book.* Garden City (N.Y.): Doubleday, 1975.

Chapin, Kim. *Fast as White Lightning.* New York: Dial, 1981.

Cutter, Robert, and Bob Fendell. *The Encyclopedia of Auto Racing Greats.* Englewood Cliffs (N.J.): Prentice-Hall, 1973.

Engel, Lyle Kenyon. *Stock Car Racing U.S.A.* New York: Dodd, Mead and Co., 1973.

Fielden, Greg. *Forty Years of Stock Car Racing, Vol. 1, The Beginning: 1949–1958, Revised Edition.* Pinehurst (N.C.): Galfield, 1990.

——. *Forty Years of Stock Car Racing, Vol. II, The Superspeedway Boom, 1959–1964.* Pinehurst (N.C.): Galfield, 1988.

——. *Forty Years of Stock Car Racing, Vol. III, Big Bucks and Boycotts, 1965–1971.* Surfside Beach (S.C.): Galfield, 1989.

——. *Forty Years of Stock Car Racing, Vol. IV, The Modern Era, 1972–1989.* Surfside Beach (S.C): Galfield, 1990.

——. *Forty Years of Stock Car Racing, Forty Plus Four, 1990–1993.* Surfside Beach (S.C.): Galfield, 1994.

Fielden, Greg. *High Speed at Low Tide.* Surfside Beach (S.C.): Galfield, 1993.

——. *Real Racers: Heroes and Record Writers from Stock Car Racing's Forgotten Era.* Surfside Beach (S.C.): Galfield, 1998.

——. *Rumblin' Ragtops: The History of the NASCAR Fabulous Convertible and Speedway Division.* Pinehurst (N.C.): Galfield, 1990.

Fleischman, Bill, and Al Pearce. *The Unauthorized NASCAR Fan Guide '99.* Farmington Hills (Mich.): Visible Ink Press, 1999.

Fleischman, Bill, and Al Pearce. *Inside Sports NASCAR Racing.* Detroit: Visible Ink Press, 1998.

Golenbock, Peter. *American Zoom.* New York: McMillan, 1994.

——. *The Last Lap.* New York: McMillan, 1998.

Higgins, Tom, and Steve Waid. *Junior Johnson: Brave in Life.* Phoenix: David Bull, 1999.

Higgins, Tom. *NASCAR's Greatest Races.* New York: HarperEntertainment, 1999.

Hunter, Don, and Al Pearce. *The Illustrated History of Stock Car Racing.* Osceola (Wis.): MBI, 1998.

Hunter, Jim. *Darlington Raceway 50th Anniversary.* Charlotte (N.C.): UMI, 1999.

Hunter, Jim, and David Pearson. 21 *Forever: The Story of Stock Car Driver David Pearson.* Huntsville (Ala.): Strode, 1980.

Irvan, Ernie, and Peter Golenbock. *No Fear.* New York: Hyperion, 1999.

Kirkland, Tom and David Thompson. *Darlington International Raceway 1950–1967.* Osceola (Wis.): MBI, 1999.

Latford, Bob. *Built for Speed. The Ultimate Guide to Stock Car Racetracks.* Philadelphia: Courage, 1999.

Sowers, Richard. *The Complete Statistical History of Stock-Car Racing.* Phoenix: David Bull, 2000.

Yarborough, Cale, and William Neely. *Cale: The Hazardous Life and Times of the World's Greatest Stock Car Driver.* New York: Times Books, 1986.

Index

About the Author

Jim McLaurin writes about auto racing for *The State* of Columbia, South Carolina. He won the writer-of-the-year awards of the National Motorsports Press Association in 1993 and 1999 and of the International Hot Rod Association in 1983.